Sodom, U.S.A.

By Christopher L. Gregory

Scripture quotations are from the NEW KING JAMES VERSION.

ISBN 1-4538-8640-0

CONTENTS

Chapter One

A brief history of perversion

A large crowd gathered together on the steps of the California State Courthouse on Tuesday, June 15th 2008. Many held signs which read, "Don't take away my right to marry!" and "Keep your religion out of our bedroom". Many shouted chants and obscenities toward those who had gathered across the street, partially blocked by the hundreds of body armored sea of police and swat teams as both crowds began to grow in size and in number.

On the opposition side of the political spectrum were celebrities of well known television programs and talk shows such as; Ellen Degeneres and her partner, Portia de Rossi, Drew Barrymore, Kathy Griffin and her mother Maggie Griffin, Star Trek's George Takei and husband Brad Altman, Kelly Osbourne and finance Luke Worrell, Deborah Gibson, Emmy Rossum, Sophia Bush, Perez Hilton and Shanna Moakler.

The cries of outrage seemed to grow, often with violent intensity and fervor as the seemingly displeased group of gatherers echoed their disapproval of the recent court decision.

What had occurred that morning was the California Supreme Court had decided in favor of proposition eight, a provision that voters decided on which made gay marriage almost impossible in the State. The court upheld prop 8 and thus practically cementing the idea that marriage was between a man and a woman and not of homosexual relationships. The ruling was a victory to those who upheld the sanctity of marriage and morality but a political tool in the future to those who were bent on changing the idea of marriage to a more open and alternative lifestyle for many.

When the courts ruled in favor of traditional marriage, it signaled a virtual war of morality not only in the State of California, but in the entire nation. The die had virtually been cast for a much bigger battle, one which will be fought in churches, synagogues, schools and homes as the defense of traditional marriage has been all but challenged and a line drawn for morality in America. This will be our last and greatest battle that the church, as well as our nation, will face in the near future.

But what started this course of events in our nation's history?

In the first half of the 20th century, people, looking for better opportunities than the dust bowls of the plains and the farm crisis in the Midwest could give them, sought their glimmer of hope in the large cities of America such as New York, Los Angeles and San Francisco. Once there, they were often forced to live outside traditional family structures, many in same sex settings such as military and industrial barracks, for prolonged periods. Those with homosexual inclinations found one another at the same time that they found the freedom to express themselves without ever-present familial and religious disapproval. For women in particular this was a new experience.

But in addition to economics changes, another extremely significant factor in the

development of coastal gay and lesbian enclaves was the ban on gays in the military. After W.W.11 thousands of gay and lesbian people were dishonorably discharged from the armed services, and many were simply dumped in port cities. At times several hundred ex-service people were deposited in San Francisco per day. They couldn't go home in disgrace, so they stayed.

The Mattachine Society drew tremendous support after one of its founders, Dale Jennings, was arrested for "lewd and dissolute behavior" in February 1952. Jennings took the unheard course of acknowledging his homosexuality in court while pleading innocent to the charges against him, thus forcing authorities to draw a distinction between being homosexual and being guilty of illegal activity. The jury was deadlocked and a retrial ordered, but the DA's office dropped all charges. Publicizing this victory wasn't easy, however. There was a news blackout on all the information regarding homosexuality; no press releases were accepted by any newspapers, magazines, or radio stations. The Mattachine Society was forced to circulate information solely through postings and flyers distributed in areas where homosexuals were believed to congregate. Nevertheless, the event drew tremendous, if quiet, support, and membership in the Mattachine Society grew by several thousand in succeeding weeks.

Fears generated by Joseph McCarthy's campaign to rid America of Communists eventually led to the neutralization of the Mattachine Society. By late 1954 it was the weak, fully public, as similationist organization whose main purpose was to convince heterosexuals that homosexuals presented no threat whatsoever to any of their values and were in fact exactly like them but for sexual preference. The lesbian organization Daughters of Bilitis, founded in San Francisco in 1955, didn't fare much better, although both groups managed to sustain publications with national circulation through the 1950's and 60's. By 1969 there were about fifty "homophile" organizations in the US, all fairly small.

The main reason for the lack of visibility in post-war America was spirit filled Biblical churches who took a stand on immorality in their congregations as well as personal life. Non celibate gay people were rightfully condemned by the holiness churches and their lifestyles unwelcome in most mainstream religious organizations not only as leaders but even simply as members. Churches who were filled with the power of God, took a stand against immorality and sin. This strong stand against sin and perversion by many churches and larger denominations, led the Reverend Troy Perry, a Baptist who himself was found to be involved in a homosexual relationship in his own church he pastured, to found the Metropolitan Community Church in 1968. Today the MCC is the largest gay and lesbian religious organization in this country and by far the largest in the South.

The first known homosexual political organization in the U.S. was the Mattachine Society, founded in November of 1950 in Los Angeles. This underground emancipation movement was the brainchild of Harry Hay, a young musicologist who had honed his organizing skills in the ranks of one of the most underground political movements in America in this century, the Communist Party. As Hay well knew, persecution of homosexuals was rampant. Police constantly entrapped and brutalized gay people. Public disclosure of homosexuality was enough to get most people fired from their jobs and ostracized from families and communities. By early 1953 under President Eisenhower homosexuality became, by executive order, a necessary and sufficient reason in itself to fire any federal employee from his or her job. Most defense industries and others with government contracts followed suit. Through the early 1970s gay and lesbian communities pushed for anti-discrimination laws, and they were successful in a few cities with little to no opposition from Christian groups and organization. Once again the church had lost an opportunity to stop a swelling tide of perversion and immorality. By 1977 California even had its first openly gay elected official; Harvey Milk was elected San Francisco City Supervisor from District 5. But it was also in 1977 that Anita Bryant began her anti-gay campaign in Dade County, Florida, which was calculated to repeal Miami's legal protections for gay citizens. Throughout 1977 there were successful referenda to repeal gay rights laws across the country-in St. Paul, Wichita, and Eugene.

In 1978 California state senator John Briggs introduced a move to prohibit homosexuals from teaching in California public schools. The initiative was defeated in November after a series of statewide debates between Briggs and Harvey Milk. It looked like gay rights would hold firm in California, but less than three weeks later Harvey Milk and pro-gay San Francisco mayor George Mascone lay dead, assassinated by former city supervisor Dan White. A jury subsequently gave White the lightest possible sentence on a charge of manslaughter. San Francisco's gay population rioted; but the heyday of pro-gay politics was over in that city and anti-gay violence sky-rocketed.

Not long after, scientists at the Centers for Disease Control began to notice a number of

Immune-deficiency-related illnesses in the gay male populations of major cities. Public

Officials (who didn't know what caused the illnesses or exactly how they were spread) began closing down establishments where gay people gathered. Not surprisingly, gay people resisted these moves, seeing them as just another ploy on the part of politicians and police to destroy gay communities and to oppress individuals. Tensions between gay communities and various branches of government increased.

In 1986 in Bowers v. Hardwick the U.S. Supreme Court held that states have a right to

Criminalize even private and consensual sexual behavior. Specifically the court said Georgia had a right to punish Michael Hardwick for sodomy even though his act occurred in private.

The police officer who over-heard and then witnessed Hardwick's act had entered the house in order to speak to one of Hardwick's housemates about a traffic violation. Officer Bowers placed Hardwick under arrest in his own bedroom.

The following year, 1987, the second March on Washington was held. It was one of the largest civil rights demonstrations in this country's history, drawing more than 650,000. The next day 5,000 demonstrators converged on the Supreme Court steps, and an organization new even to most lesbian and gay Americans, ACT-UP, made its first national appearance.

There are efforts in dozens of states and localities to repeal anti-discrimination laws where they exist and to prohibit them where they don't yet exist so that non-heterosexual people will have no avenue for changing the laws that affect them.

In the late Eighties State legislatures began to shift their support of morals in favor of a more contemporary and more liberal policy than their predecessors who espoused a more Biblical traditional view of marriage and homosexuality.

In 1990, three states Texas, Kentucky, and Michigan repealed their laws outlawing homosexual practices.

By 2000 28 states, homosexual practices are legal, six outlawed certain "deviate" practices - (sodomy).

June 2003: 4 states still criminalize homosexual sodomy

June 2003: Lawrence v. Texas- Supreme Court overturns 1986 Bowers v. Hardwick: States cannot criminalize homosexual sodomy, specifically

At the present time 87 cities or countries have passed ordinances prohibiting discrimination on the basis of sexual orientation.

Nine states also extend legal civil rights protection to gays.

: Canadian Parliament "endorses" gay marriage. USA--evenly split?

But, some jurisdictions (Cincinnati) specifically prohibit laws from being passed that protect homosexuals from discrimination.

Nationally, a majority of Americans favor the passage of equal-rights laws protecting homosexuals against job discrimination, by a margin of almost two to one - 62% favor, 32% oppose.

What started out as a mere spiritual issue had begun to take on a new meaning as the interest in perverse sexual behavior became common in many growing circles and communities. What was considered immoral was now thought to be nothing more than an alternate lifestyle. Even Hollywood began to explore the depths of depravity with such early films as "The Boys in the Band, Victor/Victoria, Making Love, Personal Best, Deathtrap, and Partners." But it was the 2006 Hollywood sleeper, "Broke back Mountain." That would break the traditional ideas of homosexuality in favor of a more tolerant perception of a homosexual lifestyle. The movie would go on to earn eight Oscars and usher in such notable homosexual actors and directors such as Harvey Fierstein and John Waters and once again place a perverse image of sexual immorality into the public mainstream. Homosexuality was now in full bloom and sadly the church was no where to be found.

Chapter Two

The seeds of abomination take root

"The purpose of education and the schools is to change the thoughts, feelings and actions of the student." Benjamin Bloom.

It has been often said that the way to change a nation is not thru force or intimidation, but thru the mind of a child. For years America had educated its young people for preparation for a soviet threat thru communism. Years of teaching and training about American values were applied to students; constant sermons of the benefits of capitalism and American ingenuity were shared by most, if not all, of teachers and professors. But while our schools were busy wailing against the dangers of communism, another, more dangerous threat was taking seed in the hearts of many.

It wasn't being taught by most teachers nor was it being offered as a secondary requirement for learning, no, this was being taught by a more enticing educator, whose grasp upon the youth would quickly take control as a more viable solution to indoctrination, it was pleasing to the eyes and soothing to the lips. With names such as Madonna, Michael Jackson, George Michael and Britney Spears, their message would be more receptive and find a nerve with most young people who listened. And they did listen.

The message was obviously clear; it was okay to be sexually open to new ideas. Once the MTV generation began to accept this new open behavior that was once considered wrong, immoral and damaging to ones health, more and more educational directors began seeing an opportunity that they had for years only dreamt about, the tide was turning in their favor to esponge their ideas into the hearts and minds of our children.

In Cambridge, Massachusetts school officials began to organize a new program dealing with alternative lifestyles, it was called, "Gay and Lesbian pride day", their main focus was not middle school or High School students, their message, a message of tolerance and understanding of homosexuals were given to elementary children as young as five years old.

The principal noted that this new program was a way to establish a new bridge to help young children come to an understanding that homosexuality is not only healthy, but also a realistic part of our culture. The principal went on to state that he did not feel that it was appropriate that values be taught only at home, but there were social values as well, even community values that only a school could give. This idea is more than alarming, it's frightening! The harm being done is enormous.

The reality is that the more children who are indoctrinated by alternative lifestyle propaganda, the more the child will feel compelled to accept, usually by peer pressure and social efforts, a more open tolerance and acceptance of a homosexual and their practices. Another reality is even more shocking and one to be taken very serious as it relates to children who are educated in alternate lifestyle programs. Based on current statistics, there is a 70-80 percent chance that a [Christian] child will abandon the church and their faith in a public school setting that promotes immoral teachings.

But still the real threat of indoctrination has begun. On June 29, 2009 San Francisco Bay-area Alameda Unified School District has approved a "lesbian, gay, bi-sexual and transgender" (LGBT) curriculum for use with kindergarten through fifth-grade students. The curriculum is intended to deal with issues such as bullying and harassment.

In Vermont students were given a course in what was being called, "Gendertopia". In this after school event, students were asked to take photos around town and then discuss the different ways gender is portrayed. The goal of the class is to make the children aware of the different types of gender beyond male and female.

Even Ohio State University freshmen are now required to undertake a first year course in what is being billed as a, "Diversity Seminar" that reflects the different groups and social communities found not only on campus but in their communities. With a focus on homosexual tolerance and acceptance, the University hopes to bring a new heightened outlook on the continuing changes taking place in American values and demographics, namely those who live an alternative lifestyle.

The Bible warns us of what would happen to a nation that forgets God. The reproach (i.e., disgrace and shame) openly being manifested in America today is indicative of the fact that we are quickly becoming a nation without God. Frankly, what this means is that the continued existence of this country is at stake. It may be that God usually judges individuals at the end of time, but the Bible clearly teaches that He judges nations in time. In Romans 1, the apostle Paul gives the four step decline in the history of the nation that forgets God:

1. A nation rejects God,

2. It turns to false religion,

3. It becomes bogged down in immorality and violence,

4. And then God judges it.

Consequently, a nation without God is a nation in serious trouble.

It is astonishing to anyone with any sense of Biblical foundation can see that our nation is in moral decay, but it seems as if no one is acknowledging this, especially the church! How prevalent is the homosexual lifestyle in America? A recent article in Time magazine suggests that it is very prevalent. In 1948, Sexologist Alfred Kinsey published figures that homosexuals found cheering. He estimated that 4% of American white males are exclusively homosexual and that about two in five had "at least some" homosexual experience after puberty. Given Kinsey's naive sampling methods, the figures were almost certainly wrong. But chances are that growing permissiveness about homosexuality and a hedonistic attitude toward all sex have helped "convert" many people who might have repressed their inclinations in another time or place.

This epidemic, which God calls an "abomination" [Lev. 18:22], has become celebrated among many and tolerated by others who have forgotten the stance God has placed on certain sexual sins – especially the sin of homosexuality.

How can it affect a nation or a people? Let's look directly to the word of God for that answer.

Jude 7 records that Sodom and Gomorrah "acted immorally and indulged in unnatural lust." Ezekiel says that Sodom committed "abominable things" (Ezek. 16:50), which referred to homosexual and heterosexual acts of sin. Lot even offered his two virgin daughters in place of his guests, but the men of Sodom rejected the offer, preferring homosexual sex over heterosexual sex (Gen. 19:8–9). Ezekiel does allude to a lack of hospitality in saying that Sodom "did not aid the poor and needy" (Ezek. 16:49). So homosexual acts and a lack of hospitality both contributed to the destruction of Sodom, with the former being the far greater sin, the "abominable thing" that set off God's wrath.

God appeared to Abraham while he lived in Mesopotamia, calling him to leave his native land and go to a place that God would allow him. Along with Abraham went his father and his nephew Lot. Lot, himself, had not heard God's call, but followed his uncle, who had heard from god. Lot was good in this regard because he not only followed his uncle, but he himself became a righteous man. Abraham, an older believer was able to disciple Lot as a disciple of the same faith in God. The beginning of those two men was indeed most encouraging. Later on however they separated and their spiritual paths diverged greatly. Why?

The choice of Lot.

Lot chose Sodom for it seemed good to him to dwell in that particular area of land, but God did not nor felt that it was a good place for him to be, but Lot carried on, separating from Abraham and residing in the land of Sodom.

How is this relevant to the church? It's relevant on many levels. The church today is divided on it's stance on morality, doctrinal issues and direction. One would be hard pressed to find two born again believers who would agree on anything much less on the weather, but the fact remains, the church, as well as the nation itself is at the place where Abraham and Lot were at. A decision will be made, it's already being made and what is being agreed upon is not what God wants nor intends for his people.

The fact is, the church is and always will be the direction guider for any nation, but as the presence of God is being ignored, the church and the nation are at odds just as in the case of Abraham and Lot.

Abraham was the head of the household, where Lot was merely a young man. Furthermore, all the substance Lot possessed actually came through his uncle. He should not have permitted his herdsmen to quarrel with Abraham's herdsmen. Abraham realized he could not strive; and this was regarded as his victory. Lot should have conceded that he would rather let his own flocks and herds take the least productive land rather than ever leave his uncle.

They were the only family in Canaan that believed in God. How could he bring himself to leave that family? Sadly, though. Lot did not think in those terms. He considered the pasture land fro his cattle and sheep to be far more important than family unity. He should rather forfeit his cattle and sheep. But what was even worse was that since his uncle now gave him a choice, he would rather choose the better of the two land areas and leave to his uncle the inferior one.

There was a time in our nation's history that when a nation needed direction, that our countries greatest leaders would find their guidance, not in political insiders, not thru committee meetings, polls or even special interest groups with their own agendas. Our nation's leaders would seek God first, even suggesting having certain church members pray that God would guide them into the right direction over issues that would affect millions, not only in the United States, but worldwide.

But as in the case of Lot, our nation is drifting further and further away from where God wants us to be, the land of Sodom might look greener from far away, but within it's mystical walls there thrives a darkness that God promises he will destroy and any people, nation or church that supports or desires Sodom, then God will judge that decision in his own righteous way.

The truth is, the more we grow further from God the more we begin to accept the lifestyles of those who live in Sodom. Currently the tide has shifted dramatically in the case of homosexuality and our country. With States largely supporting the rights of gay men and women to marry, to adopt, to live in a civil union has affected not only secular society, but it is affecting the church as well.

Recently Saddleback Pastor and evangelical leader – Rick Warren, publicly apologized for his former stance on homosexuality and gay marriage. I use the term (former) for it appears that even in Rick's mind, the church is doing a disservice to gay people by condemning their actions and lifestyle. But are we not called to share the gospel of Jesus Christ to a people who are living in darkness?

The apostle Paul said we are.

In his apologetic speech, Pastor Warren declared on Larry King that he never intended for his words to be twisted by conservative Christians in any political or Christian stance when it came to immorality, such as in the case of homosexuality. Warren says, "You know, Larry, there was a story within a story that never got told," he said. "In the first place, I am not an anti-gay or anti-gay marriage activist. I never have been, never will be. During the whole Proposition 8 thing, I never once went to a meeting, never once issued a statement, never – never once even gave an endorsement in the two years Prop 8 was going. The week before the – the vote, somebody in my church said, Pastor Rick, what – what do you think about this? And I sent a note to my own members that said, I actually believe that marriage is – really should be defined, that that definition should be – say between a man and a woman.

"And then all of a sudden out of it, they made me, you know, something that I really wasn't," Warren continued. "And I actually – there were a number of things that were put out. I wrote to all my gay friends – the leaders that I knew – and actually apologized to them. That never got out. There were some things said that – you know, everybody should have 10 percent grace when they say public statements. And I was asked a question that made it sound like I equated gay marriage with pedophilia or incest, which I absolutely do not believe. And I actually announced that. All of the criticism came from people that didn't know me. Not a single criticism came from any gay leader who knows me and knows that for years, we've been working together on AIDS issues and all these other things."

Everything Rick Warren says is a compromise with the world instead of presenting the gospel of salvation to the world. I find this to be true ranging across the spectrum from Rick Warren's purpose driven seeker friendly gospel light movement to his many media opportunities that never clearly presents the gospel of Christ and never speaks of man's, sin or need of repentance.

If a Christian pastor cannot stand up for clear teachings of their faith he certainly should not be standing in your church pulpit. The only reason I think Rich Warren is standing at Saddleback church is that the church membership has been made in his image. By the way, while I am at it, here is an example of how Rick Warren grows his Church.

It is amazing to me that an "Evangelical" Christian leader would actually apologize to homosexual leaders because some of them might think he took the biblical stand against homosexual perversion and marriage perversion. Also read this article that quotes what Rick Warren actually said to his church on Proposition 8. Apparently Rick Warren was even spinning the truth to Larry King about his position.

But this is one instance of how far both a nation as well as the church is failing to come to admonishing sin and sinful behavior. As the apostle Paul declares in Romans 1:26-27: "For this cause God gave them up unto vile affections: for even their women did change the natural use into that which is against nature: And likewise also the men, leaving the natural use of the woman, burned in their lust one toward another; men with men working that which is unseemly, and receiving in themselves that recompense of their error which was meet."

We are warned by Paul that the further our nation, or any nation for that matter, strays from the guidelines of the moral code he has established that he will deal harshly with that nation. Already we see the affects of judgment on our nation because of sin and its unrepentant people and yet, the church remains silent when it comes to open immorality. This can only have one outcome – judgment.

In Psalm 11:3, the question is asked, "If the foundations be destroyed, what can the righteous do?" Of course, when the foundations are destroyed, the righteous are made a prey of the wicked.

The reproach (i.e., disgrace and shame) openly being manifested in America today is indicative of the fact that we are quickly becoming a nation without God. Frankly, what this means is that the continued existence of this country is at stake. It may be that God usually judges individuals at the end of time, but the Bible clearly teaches that He judges nations in time. In Romans 1, the apostle Paul gives the four step decline in the history of the nation that forgets God:

1. A nation rejects God,

2. It turns to false religion,

3. It becomes bogged down in immorality and violence,

4. And then God judges it.

Consequently, a nation without God is a nation in serious trouble.

As a people (I'm speaking now of God's people), let us be actively engaged in doing justice and righteousness, and let us be praying that there is still enough salt left to preserve the blessings of God upon this nation. For I fear as the times grow darker, the epidemic of sin shall make our nation weak and Godless.

Chapter Three

Homosexuality 101

When we think about homosexuality we are to question why people, regardless of color, gender or race or even religious belief, would accept and become part of this lifestyle. What is it about this sin that many feel "compelled" to be apart of, even defend?

I believe if we look more at the spiritual aspect of this sin, we will come to see what God would have revealed to us in why so many people, sons, daughters, parents have been caught up in this lifestyle and more importantly, what the solution is. Obviously, to the Christian, the answer and the solution will always be Jesus Christ and the cross!

What is sexual orientation?

This is the word used to describe a person's romantic, emotional, or sexual attraction to another person. A person who is attracted to another of the same sex is said to have a homosexual orientation, commonly referred to as gay (for both men and women) and lesbian (for women only). Those with an attraction to persons of either, or both, sexes are considered bisexual. Those with an attraction to persons of the other sex are considered heterosexual (slang word is "straight").

Is homosexuality a mental illness?

No. It is a spiritual illness. All of the leading professional mental health organizations have publicly affirmed that homosexuality is not a mental illness. The Diagnostic and Statistical Manual of Mental Disorders is the guide in which mental health professional's turn, to identify and label human behavior as disordered. In 1973, the experts found that homosexuality does not meet the criteria necessary to be considered a mental illness.

What determines our sexual orientation?

Homosexuality is defined as a same-sex sexual activity. We as Christians believe that homosexuality is ultimately a choice that young people and adults make, just as men and women who are considered "straight" make when it comes to normal sexual "sin", the decision is the same, and it's a decision to sin. Although many young adults who decide to "explore" their sexuality, they are often heavily influenced to make this choice by bad parenting and/or sexual molestation during childhood. Media propaganda also plays a large part in sexual orientation. "Bruno" "Ellen" and many other Hollywood celebrities, make homosexuality as a normal practice. The shock of seeing Britney Spears kissing Madonna in a moment of sexual gratification on stage at the MTV music awards would have been considered too shocking for television twenty years ago, but with more and more teens and young adults being desensitized by films, reality shows and the impact MTV has played in the course of America's role in what is considered "normal" sexual behavior, young people are being sent a double sided message, an alarming message which says that sexual exploration is a good thing to be explored and understood.

The world says that no one knows what causes a person to become heterosexual, homosexual, or bisexual. There have been research attempts made to explain the etiology of homosexuality, but just as we can not explain why roughly ten-percent of the population is left-handed, we have also come up empty each time attempts have been made to explain the roots of homosexuality. But the Bible makes it clear that while we were yet in our mother's womb he knew us. God gave us all an identity; he gave us feelings, emotions and passions.

But Satan has twisted what is considered to be normal sexual behavior to one of perversion. Liberal Christians, progressive Christians, secularists, gays, lesbians, bisexuals, human sexuality researchers, mental health professionals, etc. believe that there are three normal, natural and non-disordered sexual orientations: heterosexuality, homosexuality and bisexuality. Homosexuality is defined as a sexual attraction to members of the same sex. They believe that homosexual orientation is fixed early in life, perhaps before birth and perhaps at conception. Being an orientation, it is rarely if ever changeable. This is the lie the world would tell us, even liberal Christians who have forsaken the word of God, but God makes it clear his position about homosexuality and those who would disobey his commandments to abstain from its practice.

Do you not know that the wicked will not inherit the kingdom of God? Do not be deceived: Neither the sexually immoral nor idolaters nor adulterers nor male prostitutes nor homosexual offenders (1 Corinthians 6:9)

Before they had gone to bed, all the men from every part of the city of Sodom--both young and old--surrounded the house. They called to Lot, "Where are the men who came to you tonight? Bring them out to us so that we can have sex with them." Lot went outside to meet them and shut the door behind him and said, "No, my friends. Don't do this wicked thing. (Genesis 19:4-7)

While they were enjoying themselves, some of the wicked men of the city surrounded the house. Pounding on the door, they shouted to the old man who owned the house, "Bring out the man who came to your house so we can have sex with him." The owner of the house went outside and said to them, "No, my friends don't be so vile. Since this man is my guest, don't do this disgraceful thing. (Judges 19:22-23)

In a similar way, Sodom and Gomorrah and the surrounding towns gave themselves up to sexual immorality and perversion. They serve as an example of those who suffer the punishment of eternal fire. (Jude 1:7)

Therefore God gave them over in the sinful desires of their hearts to sexual impurity for the degrading of their bodies with one another. They exchanged the truth of God for a lie, and worshiped and served created things rather than the Creator--who is forever praised. Amen. Because of this, God gave them over to shameful lusts. Even their women exchanged natural relations for unnatural ones. In the same way the men also abandoned natural relations with women and were inflamed with lust for one another. Men committed indecent acts with other men, and received in themselves the due penalty for their perversion. (Romans 1:24-27)

Is it possible for someone to change his or her sexual orientation from a homosexual to become heterosexual?

With man it's not possible. But with God anything is possible to those who believe. Sin separates man from God – all sin. This includes the sin of sexual fornication – including homosexuality!

The Bible teaches that homosexuality is a sin according to several New Testament passages such as Romans 1:26-32 and 1 Corinthians 6:9. In that regard, homosexuality is no different from any other sin. If one lives a life of sin then one cannot expect to be saved as the wages of sin are death (Romans 6:23). It is only when one repents of sin and is converted that one may come into a state of salvation (Acts 3:19). This requires one to be baptized to be forgiven of sin (Acts 2:38, Romans 6: 1-11, Colossians 2: 11-13). In that regard, a person who has lived the life of a homosexual, but has repented and stopped living that life, may be saved (see 1 Corinthians 6: 9-11). However, if one is living the life of a homosexual and is unrepentant of such a life, then eternal death is the only reward that he can expect from God (Revelation 21:8).

The main reason why homosexuality is permissive in today's culture is because of willful sin. Sin in any shape or form is contrary to God's divine purpose and/or plan in one's life. Sin brings death. And it is the sin of homosexuality that is leading so many to a dark and distorted world view when they allow themselves to participate in actions which goes against God's universal laws of sin and sanctification.

The other core problem of why homosexuality is so pervasive is due to the lack of Godly preaching in most churches today! When the church stops preaching Godly behavior, when the church stops preaching about holiness, about worldliness and no longer desires to preach the standards God has given us to walk in, then we set ourselves up for a culture who does not know God, they know nothing of his righteousness nor of his holiness. When the church stops standing in the gap against sinful standards, then it can be assumed that sooner or later that nation and its people will fall into moral decay. It's simply a matter of time. I believe we are now seeing the fruits of our failure as a church who is supposed to stand up for moral righteousness.

Chapter Four

Born or manufactured?

For the purpose of this chapter I will call his name "Marsha", although Marsha is not his real name, it will serve a purpose in the next few pages which deal with the idea that homosexuals are "born that way".

So, who is "Marsha"? Marsha was born Samuel Jenkins, a 21 year old boy from Wisconsin who attends Clemson University. For years Samuel had considered himself a girl, Samuel describes growing up as a boy, despite always feeling that he was truly a girl in a recent article with MSNBC, Samuel took the unusual step that most so called, "gender confused" people take and that is taking medical treatments to re-fix their feelings of gender confusion. Samuel, with approval of both parents began a journey of leaving his past as a healthy, viable and productive young man to becoming a woman.

Most transgender stories begin with something along the lines of, "Even at my earliest memories, I knew something was not quite right." But is this true, as in the case of "Marsha"? The Bible tells us a totally different story altogether.

"I knew you before I formed you in your mother's womb. Before you were born I set you apart and appointed you as my prophet to the nations." Jeremiah 1:5

God made the order of each person, even before they were conceived as we know it, God designed each living person of who they were, their nature, their sexual orientation, their gifts and natural abilities as well as their sex. God designed each and every person from the moment of conception on how they would be when they began that magical journey of being born. But lies and distortions of truth have made the lie of gender confusion an acceptable one to many who have been decieved by this demonic doctrine. And this is exactly what it is – a lie from hell itself!

Well, first, it isn't science that determines gender. God creates man and woman and assigns distinctive biological traits and gender roles (see Genesis 1 and 2). It is we who turn this inside-out with our misguided and sinful conceptions of the alleged fluid and subjective nature of sexual identity. Such gender confusion is called an "abomination" in Scripture (Deut. 22:5).

What man has done, being led by selfish and wicked behavior, is to allow such ideas into the mainstream public where people who are hurting and lonely and desperate for a relationship are given false ideas and false philosophies thereby distorting their original question of why they are feeling the way that they do.

Is there any doubt that we are living in an era of sexual and gender confusion? In our post-modern mind, we ourselves determine what it means to be man and woman, to be human. The Author of creation is cast aside as the goddess science is enthroned and worshipped, even in the "church."

Of course, such a thorough-going rejection of Genesis 1 and 2 begins by tossing aside biblical prescriptions concerning church leadership. This distortion of spiritual origin of what God decrees as natural versus what godless science has to say was simply a necessary first step in undermining biblical authority. The wholesale rejection of biblical manhood and womanhood within the culture has largely been accepted within the institutional church.

Take as one example the leadership of Willow Creek Community Church, one of America's largest and most influential evangelical bodies. In January, 1996, John Ortberg, then a teaching pastor at Willow Creek, authored a position paper distributed to staffers at the Illinois mega church. Mr. Ortberg wrote that on the issue of gender equality, the church "has sought to insure an appropriate level of consensus on this issue with new staff members" in order to avoid a divisive environment that "would be destructive to authentic community and effective ministry." Ortberg goes on to say that "when the Bible is interpreted comprehensively, it teaches the full equality of men and women in status, giftedness and opportunity for ministry."

Christians who aren't embarrassed by their Bibles might beg to differ, and can claim the authority of the Apostle Paul:

If anyone sets his heart on being an overseer, he desires a noble task. Now the overseer must be above reproach, the husband of but one wife, temperate, self-controlled, respectable, hospitable, able to teach, not given to drunkenness, not violent but gentle, not quarrelsome, not a lover of money. He must manage his own family well and see that his children obey him with proper respect. (If anyone does not know how to manage his own family, how can he take care of God's church?) He must not be a recent convert, or he may become conceited and fall under the same judgment as the devil. He must also have a good reputation with outsiders, so that he will not fall into disgrace and into the devil's trap. Deacons, likewise, are to be men worthy of respect, sincere, not indulging in much wine, and not pursuing dishonest gain. They must keep hold of the deep truths of the faith with a clear conscience. They must first be tested; and then if there is nothing against them, let them serve as deacons. In the same way, their wives are to be women worthy of respect, not malicious talkers but temperate and trustworthy in everything. A deacon must be the husband of but one wife and must manage his children and his household well. Those who have served well gain an excellent standing and great assurance in their faith in Christ Jesus (I Tim. 3:1-13).

The elimination and obliteration of distinctions between the sexes and the promotion of "transgenderism" is rooted in rebellion against God's order. Indeed, such egalitarianism denies the very principle of order and attempts to arrange creation on its own terms. Equality thus becomes a philosophical and religious faith that demands the fidelity of every individual and institution. And since "conservative" evangelicals have been loath to do battle with the egalitarian ethos in our homes and churches, why are we surprised at the confusion endemic in our culture?

Where are the pastors, teachers and evangelists who will have the courage to proclaim the full counsel of God and call this confusion what the Bible deems it--an "abomination"? Where are the teachers who will call the doctrines of equality and radical transgender support what they are—heresy?

But the question remains, are they born that way or is it a mere glamorous attempt to popularize a lifestyle that is contrary to God's devine will?

The answer is found in the word of God.

"For this reason God gave them over to degrading passions; for their women exchanged the natural function for that which is unnatural, Who changed the truth of God into a lie, and worshipped and served the creature more than the Creator, who is blessed for ever. Amen. For this cause God gave them up unto vile affections: for even their women did change the natural use into that which is against nature: And likewise also the men, leaving the natural use of the woman, burned in their lust one toward another; men with men working that which is unseemly, and receiving in themselves that recompense of their error which was meet And even as they did not like to retain God in their knowledge, God gave them over to a reprobate mind, to do those things which are not convenient;" Romans 1:22-28.

From a direct quote from Devvy regarding the popular idea of social gender confusion and it's impact on society and the homosexual agenda. "Today, if you don't accept the sexual deviant agenda, you should be put in rehab and if you think I'm kidding, recall the flap over Isaiah Washington calling a cast member from some garbage program called, Grey's Anatomy, a faggot, should bring things into focus. Fellow cast member, Katherine Heigl, publicly commented that Washington should just shut up his mouth and go to rehab so he can "learn to think the right way." Joseph Goebbels, Hitler's Minister of Propaganda, would have been proud of Ms. Heigl. You either think the "right way" or off to the indoctrination camps; today it's called rehab.

This issue isn't about tolerance or discrimination. It's about science. There isn't a scintilla of scientific evidence to prove any human is born homosexual or lesbian. It's all been debunked. Science is the one thing advocates and participants of deviant sexual behavior refuse to discuss - they always bring it back to religion, which is much easier to attack. Advocates of sodomy and lesbian sex have tried to use the civil rights movement to give credibility to their argument. Pushing deviant sexual behavior as somehow part of a "civil rights movement" is just more clever marketing using powerful images. If you're born white, you can't change your skin color to black at will and visa versa. The same as if you're born Asian, you can't suddenly decide you might be Caucasian. We are all which ever race God has chosen for us. A must see DVD is "The Kinsey Syndrome."

Many lesbians have left their preferred life styles. Actress Anne Heche used to have sex with Ellen DeGeneres. Ms. Heche then went on to marry a man, have a child. Unfortunately, she divorced. Not to return to having sex with a female, but a with a man. So, which way was Ms. Heche born? Angelina Jolie used to have sex with a dyke. So, which way was Ms. Jolie born? Funny thing. Both Heche and Jolie left women to be with a man and become a mother. But, wait!

"It's clear that a change in sexual orientation is imaginable to more people than ever before, and there's more opportunity -- and acceptance -- to cross over the line," says Klein, noting that a half-dozen of her married female patients in the past few years have fallen in love with women. "Most are afraid that if they don't go for it, they'll end up with regrets."

The real issue is this that people are born with the same gender qualities the way God has intended, not by some post birth concept that many choose to accept and believe. The fact is, we as human beings were designed by God before we were ever formed in the womb, and there were no distortions, no imperfections, and no mistakes. God is perfect, his design is perfect, we should look toward the heavens, and the wonders of his creations stand a testament to his glory and his perfection, the same with man. We were wonderfully and fearfully made, not a chance evolutionary haphazard, we were made by an all powerful God.

But Satan and his evil scheme to twist and strip away this logic has corrupted the beauty of creation to where he has convinced many by their own selfish, sinful desires that they are flawed, they are not whole nor are they desirable, when in actuality God loves each and every one of us. But sadly, many have not chosen a path that is not God's way, nor is it a path in which God can bless, but allow those who wish to rebel, for whatever reason, to seek their own carnal, sinful desires. The idea many have chosen to accept when it comes to gender confusion is based on a lie. That's all it is – a lie.

Transgender, homosexuals make their choice of embracing sin because they want to, not because they were born that way. Are they really a lesbian; is Marsha really a girl meant to be as one even though she was born a boy? Or are they a product of years of propaganda shoved down their throat in massive doses by the media and special interest groups? We know the truth, we know the facts, society claims one thing, but God has declared what is right and true; we are born as we are born, both male and female, there are no mistakes.

We are born sinners, this is factual. We are born with a sin debt that must be paid, this also is factual. But to suggest that our sinful behavior is due to being "born" that way is a moot argument. Although we are born into sin, we have a source which conquered sin, death, hell and the grave and his name is Jesus Christ. He is our only hope for confusion and sin. For those who are caught up into this lie, this myth which tells them that they can't help being that way, we know different, for all men have sinned before God, but there is a advocate for us to those who would believe and if we accept him in our failures and our lies and our shortcomings, he is faithful and just to forgive us of our transgressions.

This is the only hope for those caught up into the lie of "gender confusion".

Chapter Five

Homosexual Hollywood

She started out as a routine stand up comic, then moving on to becoming a successful actress in her own right before making it big as a daytime talk show host. Her program enlisted the unusual antics of comedy, goof ball contests, regularly advising the nation about the importance of spaying ones pets, not to mention dancing, lot's and lots of dancing. She has grown to become a powerful ally in the war of political activists, especially in the realm of the homosexual agenda. I'm referring to Ellen Degeneres.

On May 15th, 2008 the California State Supreme Court ruled in favor of gay marriage, upon this heartbreaking news, one Ellen Degeneres immediately announced on her show that she and her life partner, Portia De Rossi would be tying the knot "as soon as possible".

The die had been virtually cast and the line drawn that the media darlings of Hollywood had one more cause to celebrate, one more perversion to support, but when the people of California adopted proposition 8 virtually all hell broke loose and then the stage was set for a virtual fight.

But in the midst of everything Hollywood continued its attack on traditional marriage by supporting and creating films and television shows which made homosexual perversion normal, all the while showing traditional and Christian characters and individuals as ignorant, intolerant and racist. The scheme was engaged and the powers that be in Tinsel town began to work on the younger mind set – the MTV, reality crowd and did they have an audience.

Hollywood has always had an impact on society behaviors.

Society today is full of ideas and ways of life for the average person to live up to. Are these principles accurate for the average person living in today's society? No, these standards are unrealistic and they are weighted by the major influence of Hollywood, such as Hollywood celebrities, television shows, and even television advertisements. These outside influences not only sway a person's normal view, but they also can damage the average person, usually woman, physically and emotionally. Hollywood's influence is not a healthy one, leading the typical person to conform to these so-called standards.
Elliot Aronson, the author of The Social Animal, defines conformity as

"a change in a person's behavior or opinions as a result of real or imagined pressure from a person or group of people" (1999, p.19). Some may say that this supposed pressure does not affect one's judgment, but indeed it does. Although it may not seem like pressure, the slightest circumstance could compel a person to conform to the dominator's way of thinking.

One of the three different responses to social influence is Identification. This is a response to social influence brought on by a person's quest to be like the influencer (Aronson, 1999). Aronson says that humans adopt a certain behavior because it creates a relationship to the people to whom we are identifying with (Aronson, 1999). Even though this "satisfying relationship" is what a person is looking for, it may not really be satisfying; it just seems to be.

Take, for example, the television show Ally McBeal. The main character, Calista Flockhart, seems to be as thin as she could possibly be without being hospitalized. Is this how the ideal woman in today's society should look? No, but because Ally McBeal is such a frequently viewed television show, more and more people want to look like, and even act like, the character Calista Flockhart plays on TV. This unhealthy look is so desirable now because it has not only been seen on Ally McBeal, but is now the look of celebrities. It has been called the "lollipop look" because these women's bodies look like sticks of a lollipop, and the pop being their heads.

As women are more likely to conform than men are (Aronson, 1999), the person's education, self-esteem, and age, all play into it. If a woman is young, with low self-esteem, she is going to be more influenced than a confident well-educated woman. Women in today's society look to the stars for guidance and tips in fashion, exercise, and dieting, because they believe that is where the role model is. What they don't understand, is that as they are in quest of these things, they are conforming to the actions of the celebrities, and destroying themselves at the same time. As Aronson believes, "If [they] find a person attractive or appealing in some way, [they] will be incline to accept influence from that person and adopt similar values and attitudes—not in order to obtain a reward or avoid a punishment, but simply to be like that person" (1999, p.35).

Another television show that causes conformity is Friends. A few years ago, Jennifer Aniston, who plays Rachel Greene, showed up on the show with a new layered haircut. This haircut took off and became known as the Rachel - do, Everyone wanted this haircut because it was the thing to do. As stated earlier, this attraction to the celebrities is, in social psychology, Identification. With Identification, the main ingredient is attractiveness. This being the attractiveness of the person that we are identifying with (Aronson, 1999). Therefore, the thoughts of an average person would be, 'since Jennifer Aniston looks so good with this haircut, so will I." And in essence this person will conform to the ideas of the celebrity.

This same use of identification goes for television commercials and advertisements. For instance, take hair dye commercials. Heather Locklear is one of the many celebrity spokeswomen for a specific line of hair color. Doesn't everybody just want to look like her? That is the idea. The hair color company uses Heather Locklear as a figure of higher status, and the typical person looks at her and wants to emulate her. "We identify with the model, we want to hold the same opinions that the model holds...Unless you have strong feelings or solid information to the contrary, there will be a tendency for you to adopt this position" (1999, p.38). And, in this case, this position is the way that Heather Locklear feels about a certain hair color.

No matter what, Hollywood celebrities have a definite impact on the rest of society. Whether it is on television or within an advertisement or commercial, it influences the people living in this society. This influence will continue to change and shape society as a whole, from one year to the next. These influences not only harm a person, but also begin to harm society as a whole.

So are many of today's established "gay" movers and shakers in Hollywood influencing our current culture? Yes they are, in a big way.

They influence the young mindset, the teens, the college crowd and those under 45. the reality is, since late 1989 Hollywood has started to produce more and more homosexually themed films, one in particular gained notoriety for it's handling of two men who find out during a camping session that they were in "love" with one another, but married with children. The film won several Oscars and began a conversation among our society about sexual feelings, infidelity and gay attraction. The filmmakers desired a product which would start a true conversation and they got one, but what did they truly accomplish?

They accomplished only a myth, like smoke and mirrors; all they had done was produce an illusion, a lie. What was seen in this one particular film was true betrayal on the families involved, lies, deceit, heartbreak and suffering. This movie reveals only a part of the devastation. It did not reveal the painful rippling effects homosexuality has on the immediate and extended family. Hollywood wants people to forget this fact and focus on a love affair.

Hollywood's main audience has always been children and young adults, the desire to influence the minds of the young has been going on since the early 60's when liberals infiltrated the Universities and Colleges of America, there were many who found that thru media one could influence more in a day than four years in a classroom setting, it would simply take more time.

A byproduct of Hollywood's own brokenness is the acclimation of the masses to the idea that homosexuality is an alternate lifestyle that should be embraced, that even the "Marlboro-man" or the sheepherder can be gay; thus sowing deeper doubts into many wives' hearts who are already untrusting of their husbands. "Anyone and everyone can be gay!" is their message. "Anyone and everyone who is insecure in their sexuality should question the 'heterosexual dominance' (the new term now used in psychology) of our culture" is the modern psychologists' plea. Satan's message has always been, "try it, you might like it." The subtleness of this message brings further destruction by propagating deception into the family unit. This should be a stark wake-up call to the Church; we must understand that there are men and women who are secretly struggling with their sexual identity. They are in pain, they are in your church and they need the kindness of God that leads to turning away from this brokenness. They need hope.

But Hollywood's goal is two things, A) influence and B) profit. If it does not make money it does not matter what kind of message it has, many within the studio system won't back it, but there are people within the system who have the power to make sure that even if the profit margin will not satisfy the bottom-line, they are persistent in their beliefs that they must change certain behaviors in society, it's simply the cost of promoting ones ideology.

I give you Rosie O'Donnell as an example.

Rosie was and is a comedian, author, former television personality and celebrity blogger. Her biggest claim to success was her very popular television show simply called The Rosie O'Donnell Show. The show debuted in 1996 to rave reviews, it seemed as though Rosie had her audience and it began to grow. The show won mulitple Emmy awards and her influence on culture was beginning to take shape. Her success in raising millions for charities was matched by her charismatic energy and for several seasons she raised hundreds of millions of dollars for children organizations and gay and lesbian causes.

But people also took notice of her ongoing attitude during the latter years of her show, one where she started to become politically motivated with her anti-war rhetoric and her growing resentment for conservative ideas. This weighed heavily on her show and her long trusted viewers. She became a polarizing figure to many and her strong opinions resulted in several notable controversies including an on-air dispute regarding the Bush administration's policies with the war in Iraq resulting in a mutual agreement to cancel her contract.

Toward the end of her television show, Rosie finally "came out" about her sexuality and thus her impact on her audiences began to wane. But her influence was still beign felt across Hollywood as more and more openly gay and lesbian people within the studio system celebrated her open wicked behavior and worked with her, tapping her for several projects, all of which I might add had to do with children.

This is the perfect example of how Hollywood has subtley infiltrated our soceity, by using popular Hollywood characters and incorporate them into programs that are directed to children. I mean, who would ever challenge Shrek? Or an animated monkey in a Disney film? Or even worse, who would force their children never to see a Pixar film about toys? The clever usage of openly gay individuals in programs aimed at children are a testament to the power Hollywood has over our own children. Afterall, kids love comic personalities and what they perform on screen, which makes it even harder to explain to these same children that even though Rosie, Ellen and others might seem funny and laughable for what they do on the movie screen, their lives are a complete darkness. This is the fantastic lie Satan has designed and is using in our society, not to the old, but to the young.

Even in the ever growing popularity of comics, homosexuality is being viewed as "normal" and engaging. Recently it was reported that several of Marvel comic super heroes are gay. DC's villains and heroes have also been created in some degree as being either bi-sexual or homosexual. The ever popular Batwoman was recently given a new look as well as a new sexual desire for other women. This would be the first of a major comic character to be openly lesbian.

So why the desire to bring in a homosexual angle in the world of comics? The reason is simple, to make homosexuality a normal, healthy life alternative to what older Americans had taught and believed to be the norm -- traditional relationships between a man and a woman. The agenda in this new desire to change the image of what is normal sexuality is to introduce children who are susceptible and who are influenced by popular culture and its characters to something new, something different – and it's working.

Even in video games, homosexuality is being promoted to influence the young who are the major buyers of such video games such as

Rock Band and Guitar Hero. In 1988, a creature in Nintendo's own Super Mario Bros. 2 the miniboss named Birdo was described in the original instruction manual as thinking he was a girl and wanting to be called "Birdetta". This was later censored by Nintendo of America in future appearances of the character. In 1992, the Enix Corporation was ordered to remove a gay bar in Dragon Warrior III, among other content changes, before the game could be sold on a Nintendo system.

A year later, Rare released Banjo-Tooie for the Nintendo 64 with a gay frog bartender named "Jolly Roger." The frog wanted Banjo and Kazooie to rescue his co-worker, Merry Maggie, a cross-dressing amphibian who appeared to be Jolly Roger's lover. Jolly Roger would return as a playable character in the Game Boy Advance game Banjo - Pilot (2005). Rare would also release Conker's Bad Fur Day (2001) for the Nintendo 64, featuring an alcoholic squirrel named Conker and his adventures in a world where all of the characters are foul-mouthed creatures who made various dirty jokes in reference to hangovers, homosexuality and oral sex. Enix re-released Dragon Warrior III for the Game Boy Color and was allowed to keep all the original content provided that the game was given a Teen rating by ESRB.

Some computer games focused on the humor value of homosexuality without employing the sissy trope. For example, in Adventure Soft's

Simon the Sorcerer series's, if Simon is ordered to proposition any male characters, he would remind you that he "prefers blondes". The games also make numerous gay jokes. For example, when two demons get stuck together with glue in the second game (from 1995), Simon remarks that their close contact looks "awfully suspicious." Simon the Sorcerer 3-D (2002) has more gay jokes, directed at a gay knight. Computer games would pepper dialogue with gay jokes, alongside the sissy characters and the situational gender inversion for comic relief. Computer games still introduce homosexuality through this comic rubic.

In Grand Theft Auto: San Andreas the police officers in San Fierro will say various things one would expect from a comical, homosexual character such as "Drop the soap, honey!", "Lets wrestle to submission!", and "I'm on you're a**, Daisy!" In this model, homosexuality is a joke, attached to gender inversion and used to denigrate the police, an enemy in the game. Grand Theft Auto III has construction workers who look like the similarly-dressed member of the Village People, who would shout quotes from YMCA and In the Navy. Other "Grand Theft Auto" titles would have obscure references to a city park where some of the adult patrons go to engage in public homosexual sex acts.

Perhaps one of the most flagrant instances of using gay or homoerotic imagery in a comedic way is the Cho Aniki series, an unusual group of games that uses such themes in such an exaggerated way that players regard it as a parody. The games, which have been released for various systems over the last decade, most often take the form of side – scrolling shooters starring Samson and Adon, two musclebound, phallic-looking characters who fire white globular shots from holes on top of their bald heads. The games were never released outside of Japan. In Japan, they are regarded as examples of the kuso-ge — or "sh** game" — genre, which are enjoyed purely for their kitschy badness.

In 2000, Capcom resuscitated this dormant theme with Resident Evil Code: Veronica, a game in the survival horror genre. The central antagonist is named Alfred Ashford; at the game's end he is revealed as a "cross-dressing freak" who is obsessed with his dead twin sister.

In the 2007 horror first person shooter, Clive Barker's Jericho, , the Ancient Roman Governor Cassus Vicus claims it had been a while since "tasting" both genders, aroused when confronting the Jericho Squad. Vicus is portrayed as overlly perverted, being morbidly obese and practicing cannibalism, sadomasochism and "blood orgies".

Where as the sissy characters were supposed to make the audience laugh, these predatory characters' homosexuality was intended to shock the audience, making them perceive the characters, and the civilization to which they belonged, as scary, perverse and immoral.

Activision released Star Trek: Voyager Elite Force for the PC and Playstation 2. In the game you could play as a male or a female, and in either case a female would flirt with you. Elite Force was notable in this regard, as the Star Trek franchise has often been criticized for its treatment of gay and lesbian characters on TV.

That same year Tri-Ace released Star Ocean: The Second Story for the Playstation. In the game you could choose to play as either Claude or Rena, and you have a Friendship and Romance level with each party member you acquire. Depending on those levels, you get about five endings. If you chose Claude, there was an ending where you go on a "man-date" with a member of your party by the name of Ashton. The date ends with Ashton's bizarre obsession of barrels. But it still does occur. One of the other possible endings is with Noelle, another male party member. He is very effeminate and certain scenes give him the possibility of being gay. If you chose Rena as your main character, you could get an ending with a female member of your party, Precis, where the two would go on a date. There is also a somewhat secret scene, where a love potion gets used on you, and Celine makes advances toward you. This is completely due to magic, and is mostly a source of comedy.

Shadows Hearts contained a homosexual character, a Chinese acupuncturist known as Meiyuan who improved the weapons of your characters and did so with more enthusiasm for the male characters. Shadow Hearts: Covenant in 2005 also featured gay characters: the two flamboyant Magimel brothers, who were a constant sight throughout the game. One was a tailor who would sew magical clothes when bribed with beefcake trading cards, the other was a vendor for items and weapons. In one optional scene toward the end of the game, a third major character was revealed to be gay; the ensuing offscreen anal sex was largely treated as disgusting, though one female player character called it "beautiful."Shadow Hearts: From the New World" again featured Gerard, but he is with his boyfriend this time, by the name of Buigen. They both are clad in biker clothing.

Also in 2001, Metal Gear Solid 2: Sons of Liberty featured a bisexual character, Vamp. The conversation in which this was revealed (by Solid Snake himself) also explains that he was the lover of Scott Dolph, a bisexual Navy commander. The game does not dwell on this point, and accepts it simply as a factor of the character. The 2005 sequel Metal Gear Solid 3: Snake Eater went further, featuring male bisexuality (Volgin and Major Raikov), and also some other sexual topics rarely touched upon in popular entertainment, such as sexual sadism (Volgin again), polyamory and Caesarean section.

But not only are video games the swelling growing segment of our pop culture who's influencing our children regarding homosexuality but the motive has been very clear – to introduce children and young teens to an alternative to their sexuality.

Even in the successful Harry Potter series, it was recently revealed by author and occult promoter J. K. Rowling, that her main character, Albus Dumbledore, mentor to the world-famous boy wizard and Hogwart's headmaster, is gay.

The obvious decision by Hollywood, its producers, its actors and writers, not to mention the many comic writers and literary minds in pop cultural literature have conceived a plan to attack traditional Christian ethics and morality and hinder the teachings of the Bible. In essence the players have been gathered, the plan has been carefully thought out and the object is clear, to implement an idea that is contrary to what God has approved of and their mission or objective has all but been declared, to manipulate the minds of today's young people.

If there was ever a time in the churches history that they need to be made aware of what's literally taking place in the hearts and mind of our children it is now. There is no reason for delay, the enemy knows full well that his time is all but grown short and it is the final hour before the return of our precious Lord and savior, but Satan also knows that if we do not act now, the only casualty that we will be dealt with is in our youth, who are being taught ungodly virtues, unethical behaviors and godless perversion. We need to stop playing church and get back to what really matters, defending our families, our communities and our nation while we still have time.

Chapter Six

Hate Speech or Truth?

NEW YORK CITY: The Rev. Joseph Jenkins was arrested today as he preached to his congregation of 500. As he said, 'The Bible says it is a sin for a man to lie with a man!' four federal undercover agents rose from their seats in the crowded church and handcuffed the pastor. He was later charged before a US Magistrate under the federal 'Hate Crimes' law.

STOCKHOLM, July 5, 2004 (LifeSiteNews.com) - Ake Green, the pastor of a Swedish Pentecostal church in Kalmar, Sweden, has been sentenced to one month in prison by a Swedish court, for inciting hatred against homosexuals. Green was prosecuted in January for "hate speech against homosexuals" for a sermon he preached last summer citing Biblical references to homosexuality.

During a sermon in 2003, Green described homosexuality as "abnormal, a horrible cancerous tumor in the body of society".

Sweden passed an equivalent to Canada's Bill C-250 last year -- a "hate crimes" law that forbids criticism of homosexuality. In a WorldNetDaily article, the author quotes from the church newspaper Kyrkans Tidning, in which the prosecutor in the case, Kjell Yngvesson, justifies the arrest of pastor Green: "One may have whatever religion one wishes, but this is an attack on all fronts against homosexuals. Collecting Bible cites on this topic as he (Pastor Green) does makes this hate speech."

More than a decade since Matthew Shepard, a gay, 21-year-old Wyoming college student, was murdered, Democrats may pass a bill in his name that would add sexual orientation and gender identity to the list of federally prosecuted hate crimes. The House passed the legislation 249-175 in late April, and the Senate could vote on a nearly identical bill as early as today.

Opponents envision a world where pastors could be arrested for preaching against homosexuality. But supporters say the bill does plenty to protect the freedoms of speech and religion.

The disputes center on a section of the bill that purports to guard constitutionally protected speech, expressive conduct, and activities. Protected activities include "the exercise of religion protected by the First Amendment and peaceful picketing or demonstration," according to the legislation. The bill also states that no one can be prosecuted solely for expressing racial, religious, political, or other beliefs. However, the bill adds that "speech, conduct or activities consisting of planning for, conspiring to commit, or committing an act of violence" is not constitutionally protected. That sentence is alarming to conservative Christian groups such as Focus on the Family and the Family Research Council, who say the law would severely hamper Christians' freedom to address homosexuality in sermons, radio programs, and other public venues.

But is the mere preaching of the word something the homosexual activists and leftists liberals truly bent on stopping? The answer can be seen in several attempts by activist Judges and lawmakers to actually make it a crime under the current hate crime bill put forth by Congress, which says that any statement or comment(s) by people who are in a position of power that can be construed as hate speech could be fined or imprisoned for up to ten years and their non profit status revoked. Obviously the pending bill would seriously damper any attempt by Christians to preach the uncompromising word of God to those who are in sin.

Ashley Horne, a federal policy analyst for Focus on the Family, said that if passed, the law could expose pastors to federal prosecution if an attendee of their church committed a crime and blamed it on sermons about homosexuality. The bill does not adequately protect Christians from gay activists, she says. She worries that the prosecution would be based on evidence of motivation.

But is the preaching against homosexuality "hate speech?"

Under the current U.S. Constitution, American citizens are protected by freedom of speech, but over time those rights have been openly challenged in the courts by radical leftist's whose sole intention is to remove and/or stop the free expression of so called, "hate speech". To be sure, this is not about merely stating a fact of disapproval of one's like ability or a "I don't like you so I'll just say it." The real issue is the agenda by many of these people who want to silence the gospel from being preached altogether. Make no mistake, Paul states it very clearly that, "For we wrestle not against flesh and blood, but against principalities, against powers, against the rulers of the darkness of this world, against spiritual wickedness in high places." Eph. 6:12

It is quite clear that those who are adamant that the preaching against homosexuality and against sin are simply being manipulated by demonic forces. It has always been Satan's desire to silence the gospel, especially when it comes to sin. The current hate crimes bill makes it easier for Satan to silence the church and those whose sole intention is to bring those bound in darkness into the light. This is what Satan fears most, that the preaching of the gospel, which breaks the yoke of sin, will convict the heart of the sinner and thus release him from the chains of sin and death.

In recent years the courts have become even more inclined to agree with those who despise the gospel. Here are some facts to consider which suggests a trend against preachers of the gospel or religious intolerance is or has been taking a foothold in our court system.

In 1942, the Supreme Court sustained the conviction of a Jehovah's witness who addressed a police officer as a "God dammed racketeer" and "a damned facist" (Chaplinksy v. New Hampshire). The Court's opinion in the case stated that there was a category of face-to-face epithets, or "fighting words," that was wholly outside of the protection of the First Amendment: those words "which by their very utterance inflict injury" and which "are no essential part of any exposition of ideas."

American Booksellers involved a First Amendment challenge to an Indianapolis civil rights ordinance that made it a crime to distribute materials that depicted women as "sexual objects for domination, conquest, or use." The Sixth Circuit Court of Appeals invalidated the ordinance calling it "thought control." The Court ruled that the First Amendment gives government no power to establish "approved views" of various subgroups of the population.

R. A. V. considered a challenge to a St. Paul ordinance punishing the placement of certain symbols that were "likely to arouse anger, alarm, or resentment on the basis of race, religion, or gender." Robert Victoria, a teenager, had been convicted of violating the ordinance after having been found to have burned a cross on the yard of a black family. The Court, in an an opinion by Justice Scalia, reversed R. A. V.'s conviction on the ground that the ordinance unconstitutionally criminalized some hurtful expression (specifically that aimed at racial and religious minorites) and not other hurtful expression (that aimed at other unprotected groups) based on the political preferences of legislators. Scalia makes clear that "fighting words" is not, as Chaplinsky had suggested, a category of speech that is wholly outside of First Amendment protection.

A year after R. A. V., the Supreme Court unanimously upheld, in Wisconsin v. Mitchell, a statute that imposed stiffer sentences for racially-motivated assaults than for other types of assaults. The Court reasoned that the statute did not violate the First Amendment because it was aimed primarily at regulating conduct, not speech.

In Virginia v Black (2003), the Court divided on the question of whether a state could prohibit cross burning carried out with the intent to intimidate. A majority of the Court concluded that, because cross-burning has a history as a "particularly virulent form of intimidation," Virginia could prohibit that form of expression while not prohibiting other types of intimidating expression. Thus, the majority found the cross-burning statute to fall within one of R. A. V.'s exceptions to the general rule that content-based prohibitions on speech violate the First Amendment. Nonetheless, the Court reversed the Virginia cross-burner's conviction because of a jury instruction that might produce convictions of cross-burners whose motivation was ideological--and not an attempt to arouse fear. Justice Thomas dissented, arguing that cross-burning is conduct, not expression, and therefore its suppression does not raise serious First Amendment issues.

Although the idea of separating clearly defined and true "hate speech" acts and words, it's becoming very clear that judges and the courts are becoming more and more intolerant of any rhetoric that would cause undue emotional stress on a person simply because they felt "convicted" of their sins when they heard the gospel being preached, in this case when it deals with homosexuality.

But why homosexuality? What is it about homosexuality in the first place that causes an entire nation to start wanting to protect it? Give it special privileges and civil rights protection?

I believe it's because it's the last true sign of a nation who's reached her end as an empire and a world power.

The U.S. Senate passed legislation July 16, 2009 to expand hate crimes protections to include homosexuals and transgendered people.

The Matthew Shepard Hate Crimes Prevention Act gained approval as an amendment to a Department of Defense authorization bill, which is expected to be voted on the week of July 20-24. The amendment would add "sexual orientation" and "gender identity" to the current categories -- such as religion and national origin -- protected from hate crimes. "Sexual orientation" includes homosexuality and bisexuality, while "gender identity," or transgendered status, takes in transsexuals and cross-dressers.

The Senate voted 63-28 to invoke cloture, or stop debate, in order to bring the hate crimes amendment up for passage. A cloture effort requires 60 votes to be successful. The amendment then was agreed to by unanimous consent.

The House of Representatives passed a similar measure -- the Local Law Enforcement Hate Crimes Prevention Act, H.R. 1913 -- with a 249-175 vote in late April.

The Southern Baptist Ethics & Religious Liberty Commission (ERLC) and others oppose such efforts to expand hate crimes protection based not only on their inclusion of categories defined by sexual behavior or identity but also concerns about the potential impact on religious freedom.

They fear the measure, combined with existing law, could expose to prosecution Christians and others who proclaim the Bible's teaching that homosexual behavior and other sexual relations outside marriage are sinful. For example, if a person commits a violent act based on a victim's "sexual orientation" after hearing biblical teaching on the sinfulness of homosexual behavior, the preacher or teacher could be open to a charge of inducing the person to commit the crime, some foes say.

The Senate approved in a 78-13 roll call before the cloture vote an amendment by Sen. Sam Brownback, R.-Kan., intended to protect the free exercise of religion and other First Amendment rights.

Brownback's amendment says such freedoms are not to be infringed on under the hate crimes measure as long as their use is not intended to plan, prepare for or incite physical violence.

"The Brownback amendment offers some needed protections for people of faith who express their faith convictions about homosexuality and certain other aberrant sexual behaviors," said Barrett Duke, the ERLC's vice president for public policy and research. "The amendment protects the pastor as long as his speech or other action was not 'intended' to lead to an act of violence. However, it does not protect a pastor from government scrutiny if a member of his congregation engages in an act of violence against someone in one of these protected groups after he has heard a negative statement from the pastor about the group. So, anyone who speaks against homosexuality or other aberrant sexual behaviors may be presumed guilty of inciting violence and be forced to prove his innocence.

"In addition, the Brownback amendment doesn't resolve other inherent problems in the bill," Duke said. "The bill still elevates homosexuality and other aberrant sexual behaviors to a specially protected class, and it still creates an opportunity for the prosecution of thought. Consequently, while we appreciate the protection that Senator

Brownback gained for people of faith, the hate crimes bill is still inappropriate legislation and should be defeated."

Peter Sprigg, the Family Research Council's vice president for policy, welcomed the Brownback amendment but told Baptist Press that "the real threat to religious liberty may not come so much from the specific application of this bill but what may follow it. This may start us on a slippery slope to more restrictions. My concern is that just like domestic partnerships have paved the way for same-sex marriage, a law against hate crimes as acts of violence may pave the way for laws against hate speech.

"You still have a problem of a lack of equal protection," Sprigg said of the bill even with the Brownback amendment. "Some victims of violent crime are being granted more rights than other victims of violent crime. Even if in the end no one is prosecuted simply for speaking against homosexual conduct, everyone who disapproves of homosexuality is stigmatized as being guilty of hatred."

The amendment also is unclear in defining who would fit the categories of "sexual orientation" and "gender identity," ERLC President Richard Land said in a July 16 letter urging Senate Minority Leader Mitch

McConnell of Kentucky to oppose the legislation. "While the American Psychiatric Association lists roughly 30 sexual orientations, including pedophilia, the term 'sexual orientation' is unspecified in the bill, and 'gender identity' is only loosely defined," Land wrote.

The Human Rights Campaign, the country's largest homosexual political organization, applauded the Senate's action on the bill.

All 28 votes against cloture on the amendment came from Republicans, including McConnell.

President Obama has expressed support for expanding hate crimes law to include homosexuals, bisexuals and transgendered people.

The Senate measure says a person commits a hate crime when he "willfully causes bodily injury to any person or, through the use of fire, a firearm, a dangerous weapon, or an explosive or incendiary device, attempts to cause bodily injury to any person, because of the actual or perceived religion, national origin, gender, sexual orientation, gender identity or disability of any person."

The penalty for a hate crime could be as much as 10 years in prison or, in some cases, up to a life sentence.

The legislation would authorize the U.S. attorney general to provide assistance to state and local officials in the investigation and prosecution of hate crimes.

The Senate approved similar hate crimes language in 2007 as part of the defense authorization measure, but it was removed from the final bill when it became clear the House would not pass it as part of the military measure.

But what about homosexuality, why is this such a fierce topic for many, against it and those who intend on participating in this lifestyle? I believe the answer lies in past civilizations and what the word of God tells us about each of these past empires who dealt with the issue of homosexuality and what happened to them when they embraced such a perverse and abominable act.

Social and cultural acceptance of the homosexual lifestyle certainly contributed to the collapse of many empires of antiquity, including the Canaanite, Persian, Assyrian, Babylonian, Greek, and Roman empires.

The behavioral similarity between these nations and their acceptance of homosexuality is undeniable to those who understand God's warning about forsaking moral principals. When the very laws of God are broken, when a nation – any nation, who forgets this fact is doomed to repeat the downward spiral of past civilizations. Please remember, God is not mocked, his righteousness will be revealed to any nation, regardless of past intentions to do good, it is when that particular nation rejects the God of Israel and the modern church and embraces that which God calls wicked and perverse. The similarities of modern America and those who went the way we are now going is frightening when you take into consideration that we have only been a nation for almost 250 years.

Senator Zell Miller of Georgia recently quoted noted historian Arnold Toynbee on the floor of the U.S. Senate as saying, "Of the 22 civilizations that have appeared in history, 19 of them collapsed when they reached the moral state America is in today." That statement is even more startling when one realizes that the statement was made some 30 years ago! If history is any teacher, one must conclude that the acceptance of homosexuality by any mainstream culture tends to doom that society!

That the United States has chosen to embrace the homosexual lifestyle by granting it legal protection, even political correctness, reveals just how depraved our once great nation has become. Should we now be shocked that homosexual marriage is on the verge of becoming a reality?

Dr. Carle Zimmerman in 1947 wrote a book called Family and Civilization. He studies the decline of several civilizations and empires. He discovered eight patterns of domestic behavior that signaled the decline of a civilization:

. The breakdown of marriage and rise of divorce.

. The loss of the traditional meaning of the marriage ceremony.

. The rise of Feminism.

. Increased public disrespect for parents and authority in general.

. Acceleration of juvenile delinquency, promiscuity and rebellion.

. Refusal of people with traditional marriages to accept their family responsibilities.

. A growing desire for and acceptance of adultery.

. Increasing interest in and spread of sexual perversions (homosexuality) and sex-related crimes.

America and Rome:

Both superpowers began as small geographical areas that, little by little, gained more land and increased the size of their respective militaries to defend these acquisitions. The U.S. began with 13 colonies and has significantly grown in size since its birth, and the Romans had spread their way across the globe. In America political divisiveness is present and issues tend to get volatile when politicians try and assert their solutions; in some ways not unlike what happened in Rome.

The Romans and the American cultures are both loosely based off the customs of other nations. Since many of the early colonists came from Europe, America's foundational culture was primarily European in its early roots; the Romans assimilated from Greek culture. Both cultures also value entertainment, games and competitions. The Romans had the coliseum and the many events that were showcased there and the U.S. highly values celebrities and sports, showcasing them. The salaries that entertainment can command is astonishing, although in all fairness, many other nations value celebrities as well, this theme seems to exist in both ancient and modern times.

Rome was riddled with pederasty (literally "boy-love"), which refers to an intimate relationship between a boy and an adult male outside his family. In the U.S. the rise of pedophilia (adult-child sex) is growing at and alarming rate.

Every historian – even modern homosexual revisionists – admit that Rome was riddled with homosexuals. Hadrian, one of the best emperors, traveled the empire with a youthful lover, Antinous. Caligula and Nero were accused of having sex with just about anyone or anything.

Here's another historical fact. Rampant homosexuality among the upper classes in Rome led to a decline in the birth rate among aristocrats and reduced the pool of leadership manpower.

In the fifth century AD, Rome was a mess. Germanic Goths overran the Northeastern Roman border in 406.

Other non-Christian tribes - Vandals, Franks, Burgundians, Lombards, Visigoths, and Ostro-goths –posed serious threats to external Roman security. Rome's internal problems made a unified response impossible.

In 410 AD, Alaric led the Visigoths into Rome and the city was taken for the first time in 1,000 years.

The Western Roman Empire fell again to the Vandals in AD 455, and again in AD 476, when Germanic tribes over-ran it.

Like Rome, our nation is facing an ever increasing threat of terrorists, domestic and international. As in Rome, even our leaders have been recently "outed" for having homosexual tendencies and relationships with male interns, some of the age of 18!

The fact is, every society that resolved to accept homosexuality denigrated to a point of virtual chaos. The ruin of these past empires should be an example to every nation and its people that the warning God gives us is clear, that any nation who allows sinful wicked behavior and allows it to go unanswered or unchallenged by the word of God will always face the wrath of a righteous God.

Chapter Seven

When a nation forgets God

As per stated in the previous chapter, every nation which fell throughout time did so because it was either a Godless nation or it fell because of ungodliness. Can the same be said of the United States of America?

When we previously discussed the fall of Rome, one of the main causes was the sin of homosexuality. But some would say, "We're not Rome, we're not an empire." True. But what constitutes an empire?

The term empire derives from the Latin imperium. Politically, an empire is a geographically extensive group of states and peoples (ethnic groups) united and ruled either by a monarch (emperor, empress) or an oligarchy. Geopolitically, the term empire has denoted very different, territorially-extreme states — at the strong end, the extensive Spanish Empuire (16th c.) and the British Empire (19th c.), at the weak end, the Holy Roman Empire (8th c.–19th c.), in its Medieval and early-modern forms, and the Byzantine Empire (15th c.), that was a direct continuation of the Roman Empire, that, in its final century of existence, was more a city-state than a territorial empire.

In the post modern 21st century many would say that we are completely different than Rome because we are not an empire. But the facts speak otherwise.

The U.S. has the highest technlogical advancement in the world compared to Japan and China, our medical facilities are the most highly advanced in the world compared to other nations. Our military advancements by far outweighs any other nation in the field of high tech advancements. Our nation is the envy of the world for our capitalist strength and even though we suffered recently a major struggle with our economy, we were able to virtually build upon our own infrustructure and already we are re-gaining our wealth while the world watches and waits once again for our failure.

Although we are not imperilistic nor do we seek to claim "empire" to our name as a nation, it is well established that the U.S. is in fact the superpower to the world. The argument then that we are not equal to Rome is moot and holds no water.

The main reason why I believe we are going the way of Rome is due to the fact that although we have no other to fear from militarily, it is our lack of morals and departure from the faith of this nations christian foundation and its full support of homosexuals that I believe prove that we are in the final days the Lord predicted would come just before his return.

Every nation who endorsed, protected and supported immorality such as the case of homosexuality fell into demise, our demise reflects the fact that we are nearer to the returning of our lord than we thought.

Twenty – five years ago homosexuality was not so much openly spoken about, but as time and morals and the lack of the church to preach against this sin loosened, the growing segment of this particular culture began to emerge and become a force, both socially, politically and now in many cases, religiously.

Paul clearly writes about the evils in the society of his day and clearly explains the Lord's mind on this matter – that the wrath of God is revealed from Heaven against all ungodliness and unrightesouness of men.

"For the wrath of God is revealed from heaven against all ungodliness and unrighteousness of men, who hold the truth in unrighteousness." Romans 1:17

Was Paul speaking about the wicked and the homosexuals and pagans of just his day? No. A further read in that scripture reveals that the Apostle Paul was speaking about a future event, a future group of people who would be witness to the second coming of the Lord, who would find themselves contending against these sins of immorality and uncleanness.

John the Baptist speaks of the Wrath to come...a future wrath... Matthew 3:7-8

(7) But when he saw many of the Pharisees and Sadducees come to his baptism, he said unto them, O generation of vipers, who hath warned you to flee from the wrath to come?

(8) Bring forth therefore fruits meet for repentance:

Jesus Christ alludes to a 'near future' wrath... Were events in 70.AD this 'wrath'? Jerusalem has to endure this 'wrath' until the times of the gentiles are fulfilled...

Luke 21:23-24

(23) But woe unto them that are with child, and to them that give

suck, in those days! for there shall be great distress in the land, and wrath upon this people.

(24) And they shall fall by the edge of the sword, and shall be led away captive into all nations: and Jerusalem shall be trodden down of the Gentiles, until the times of the Gentiles be fulfilled.

John the apostle writes here about a 'present wrath' that abides on those who believe not in The Son of God...

John 3:36

(36) He that believeth on the Son hath everlasting life: and he that believeth not the Son shall not see life; but the wrath of God abideth on him.

Paul the apostle writes about a 'Day of Wrath' that is to come...But The Lord is patient that men everywhere will repent...

Romans 2:4-6

(4) Or despisest thou the riches of his goodness and forbearance and longsuffering; not knowing that the goodness of God leadeth thee to repentance?

(5) But after thy hardness and impenitent heart treasurest up unto thyself wrath against the day of wrath and revelation of the righteous judgment of God;

(6) Who will render to every man according to his deeds:

Wrath is promised to those who obey not the truth, Jews first and then

Gentiles…Paul draws this interesting distinction between Jews and Gentiles…wrath first to the Jews and then Gentiles…interesting, in light of historic events surrounding the persecution of Jews around the world…

Romans 2:7-9

(7) To them who by patient continuance in well doing seek for glory and honor and immortality, eternal life:

(8) But unto them that are contentious, and do not obey the truth, but obey unrighteousness, indignation and wrath,

(9) Tribulation and anguish, upon every soul of man that doeth evil, of the Jew first, and also of the Gentile;

It is only Jesus Christ who can save us from the Wrath of God.

Romans 5:9

(9) Much more then, being now justified by his blood, we shall be saved from wrath through him.

A future 'Wrath of God' is promised to the children of disobedience… but the warning goes out to Christians so that they don't get deceived by sin…

Ephesians 5:5-7

(5) For this ye know, that no whoremonger, nor unclean person, nor covetous man, who is an idolater, hath any inheritance in the kingdom of Christ and of God.

(6) Let no man deceive you with vain words: for because of these things cometh the wrath of God upon the children of disobedience.

(7) Be not ye therefore partakers with them.

Paul continues to warn that the Wrath of God comes upon the children of disobedience and all who continue to sin and therefore exhorts the saints to flee sin...

Colossians 3:5-6

(5) Mortify therefore your members which are upon the earth; fornication, uncleanness, inordinate affection, evil concupiscence, and covetousness, which is idolatry:

(6) For which things' sake the wrath of God cometh on the children of disobedience:

Paul the apostle clearly writes about the 'Wrath to Come'...it is only Jesus Christ who can deliver us from the Wrath to Come...

Thessalonians 1:10

(10) And to wait for his Son from heaven, whom he raised from the dead, even Jesus, which delivered us from the wrath to come.

Interestingly Paul writes to the Thessalonians about a 'Wrath' that came upon the Jews for resisting the preaching of the gospel...Paul even is more descriptive...he says this 'wrath' came upon the Jews to the uttermost... We see that The Lord can cause His wrath to come even in the 'present' on those who resist the gospel... Was Paul speaking of the events around 70.AD?

Thessalonians 2:14-16

(14) For ye, brethren, became followers of the churches of God which in Judea are in Christ Jesus: for ye also have suffered like things of your own countrymen, even as they have of the Jews:

(15) Who both killed the Lord Jesus, and their own prophets, and have persecuted us; and they please not God, and are contrary to all men:

(16) Forbidding us to speak to the Gentiles that they might be saved, to fill up their sins always: for the wrath is come upon them to the uttermost.

The Lord has not called us as Christians to wrath but to salvation in Jesus Christ...

Thessalonians 5:9

(9) For God hath not appointed us to wrath, but to obtain salvation by our Lord Jesus Christ,

John the apostle writes about some of the events that take place when the 'future wrath' happens – the 'great day of his wrath'...

Revelation 6:16-17

(16) And said to the mountains and rocks, Fall on us, and hide us from the face of him that sitteth on the throne, and from the wrath of the Lamb:

(17) For the great day of his wrath is come; and who shall be able to stand?

John continues to write about the 'future wrath' and events that take place when it happens...

Revelation 11:18

(18) And the nationswere angry, and thy wrath is come, and the time of the dead, that they should be judged, and that thou shouldest give reward unto thy servants the prophets, and to the saints, and them that fear thy name, small and great; and shouldest destroy them which destroy the earth.

A 'Future Wrath' is promised to all those who will receive the mark of the beast...

Revelation 14:9-10

(9) And the third angel followed them, saying with a loud voice, If any man worship the beast and his image, and receive his mark in his forehead, or in his hand,

(10) The same shall drink of the wine of the wrath of God, which is poured out without mixture into the cup of his indignation; and he shall be tormented with fire and brimstone in the presence of the holy angels, and in the presence of the Lamb:

We see the 'Future Wrath of God' here....angels get ready to pour this wrath upon all children of disobedience upon the earth...

Revelation 15:7-8

(7) And one of the four beasts gave unto the seven angels seven golden vials full of the wrath of God, who liveth forever and ever.

(8) And the temple was filled with smoke from the glory of God, and from his power; and no man was able to enter into the temple, till the seven plagues of the seven angels were fulfilled.

It is Jesus Christ who is in charge of executing the Wrath of God and It is only He who can save us from the Wrath of God...Amen!

Revelation 19:15-16

(15) And out of his mouth goeth a sharp sword, that with it he should smite the nations: and he shall rule them with a rod of iron: and he treadeth the winepress of the fierceness and wrath of Almighty God.

(16) And he hath on his vesture and on his thigh a name written, KING OF KINGS, AND LORD OF LORDS.

Will a nation face wrath for it's disobedience?

The Lord does indeed reckon with societies and civilizations that turn away from The Knowledge of God, Truth, and Justice...

There is Vengeance...from The Lord...

There is Punishment...from The Lord...

There is Anger...from The Lord...

There is Indignation...from The Lord...

There is Wrath...from The Lord...on all individuals, societies, and civilizations that reject the Knowledge of God, His Truth, His Truth, and Justice.

Wrath of God against All Ungodliness...Those who hold God's Truth in Unrighteousness...

Romans 1:17

(18) For the wrath of God is revealed from heaven against all ungodliness and unrighteousness of men, who hold the truth in unrighteousness;

First stages of God's Wrath – Society is given over to uncleanness...

Romans 1: 24-27

(24) Wherefore God also gave them up to uncleanness through the lusts of their own hearts, to dishonor their own bodies between themselves:

(25) Who changed the truth of God into a lie, and worshiped and served the creature more than the Creator, who is blessed forever. Amen.

(26) For this cause God gave them up unto vile affections: for even their women did change the natural use into that which is against nature:

(27) And likewise also the men, leaving the natural use of the woman, burned in their lust one toward another; men with men working that which is unseemly, and receiving in themselves that recompense of their error which was meet.

The wrath of God seems to come in phases, at least when one reads the Roman Chapter 1. We see that the first stage is that society is given over to the very sins and practices which the bible clearly condemns.

In Rome, society became immersed in gluttony, greed, self indulgence, Senators were known to move around with young boys who served as sex slaves to the Senators, homosexuality was normal practice, wars of greed were common and society was given over to a debased mind.

The Western world is moving towards the same Roman direction. We have States in the USA that have legalized Gay Marriages, Infanticide in the form of abortion is legal and society will continue towards that path.

What we are looking at here is not just the Wrath of God on the USA and Europe alone but on every nation that turns its back on God of the Bible. This is what the Whole Book of Revelation is about, not just a Judgment on the USA but the whole world!

A Civilization that increasingly hates God...

Romans 1:28-32

(28) And even as they did not like to retain God in their knowledge, God gave them over to a reprobate mind, to do those things which are not convenient;

(29) Being filled with all unrighteousness, fornication, wickedness, covetousness, maliciousness; full of envy, murder, debate, deceit, malignity; whisperers,

(30) Backbiters, haters of God, despiteful, proud, boasters, inventors of evil things, disobedient to parents,

(31) Without understanding, covenant breakers, without natural affection, implacable, unmerciful:

(32) Who knowing the judgment of God, that they which commit such things are worthy of death, not only do the same, but have pleasure in them that do them.

Rome had become a society that increased in hatred for God. A certain Roman emperor at some point expelled Jews from Rome; he then proceeded to persecute Christians and used them as objects of game by feeding them to lions in the Roman Coliseums. Rome rejected the knowledge of God in their philosophies and became a society that hated God.

Jesus Christ told us plainly that in the last days just prior to His Second coming, there is going to be a global hate movement against True Christians...there is going to be heavy persecution globally against all those who believe in The Name of Jesus Christ.

Matthew 24:9

(9) Then shall they deliver you up to be afflicted, and shall kill you: and ye shall be hated of all nations for my name's sake.

The fact is this nation as we know it has changed within the past fifty years. Our society has changed, our morality has changed even our theology and spirituality has changed. More and more our culture is embracing that which God declares as evil, and although many in television and whose popularity rises in status might state that certain perversions are nothing more than "lifestyle" alternatives, the fact remains God will judge a nation and a people who reject his truth.

Psalm 9:17 "The wicked shall be turned into hell, and all the nations that forget God."

Chapter Eight

When the persecution starts

It was a moment that shook the world. While the world was dealing with economic issues, the U.S. embroiled in two wars, North Korea threatening to launch more missiles as a sign of its independence as Israel and Iran turned up its rhetoric to annihilate each other – and they still are of this writing, the rest of the civilized world was watching something else of universal proportions – a girl in a bikini.

Prejean attracted national attention when she answered a question at the Miss USA Pageant defending traditional marriage. The unprecedented personal attacks that ensued eventually culminated in Prejean being stripped of her Miss California crown. But the 22-year-old won the respect of millions for modeling something other than evening gowns and swimsuits—the courage of standing up for her convictions.

In 2007, speaking at a fundraising banquet for the Indiana Family Institute, then former Indianapolis Colts head coach Tony Dungy, a devout born again Christian and motivator to young people nationwide, faced an outcry of intolerance and hatred by homosexual activists when Dungy declared that marriage was between a man and a woman. He's took a little heat for it because of the organization's desire to make gay marriage illegal in the state of Indiana. The ironic thing was that many of those who objected (homosexuals) criticized the low-key coach for being prejudiced. Coach Dungy refused to apologize for his then comments and stood by his Christian views.

The agenda, it seems is clear, the point to be taken is that many who hold to traditional Christian principals are being systematically singled out for condemnation by the very ones who preach tolerance and unity. The homosexual activists have made it clear that those who would dare suggest that homosexuality is not a genetic trait, born into this perversion but simply a choice as sin always is, and should be met with scorn and hatred.

In June of 2009 Congress voted on the Matthew Shepard hate crime bill which, if passed would make it difficult for any Christian to preach against the act or lifestyle of homosexuality. The bill imposes special fines for those who commit a "hate crime" against a protected class and provides federal assistance to those prosecuting such crimes. Existing hate-crimes law provides federal help to states and localities in prosecuting crimes based only on the victim's race, religion or national origin.

Christian activists stand firm to the belief that if this measure is passed and signed into law, the legislation could be used to target Americans who voice their opposition to the homosexual lifestyle – including pastors preaching and reading the Bible.

Passage would literally throw open the door to attacks against people of faith, who could be prosecuted with federal monies for expressing their views on homosexuality!

Homosexual activists have redefined any opposition to homosexuality as 'hate speech.' Laws already criminalize speech that incites violence. It's easy to imagine a scenario in which any incident involving a homosexual can be blamed on people who have publicly opposed homosexual activism.

Because it offers special protection to specific class of people, the legislation violates the Equal Protection Clause of the U.S. Constitution. The Human Rights Campaign hailed last week's House vote.

"Congress should work to protect Americans, not discriminate against them," said HRC President Cheryl Jacques. "We laud Congress for this vote, especially Minority Leader Pelosi for offering this motion and working to get the overwhelming support of her peers. We urge conference committee members to take it to heart – keep the federal hate-crimes bill in conference committee."

According to HRC, the House passed a similar motion in September 2000 by a 232-192 vote, but that amendment was removed in conference committee. The homosexual-advocacy group claims the new hate-crimes language has been endorsed by more than 175 law-enforcement, civil-rights, civic and religious organizations.

Even more recently a new law was passed in Canada that adds sexual orientation as a protected category in the nation's genocide and hate-crimes legislation, which carries a penalty of up to five years in prison. What this new law will do that many believe is create a new law that the Bible will be deemed "hate literature". Under the criminal code in certain instances, as evidenced by the case of a Saskatchewan man who was fined by a provincial human-rights tribunal for taking out a newspaper ad with Scripture references to verses about homosexuality.

Earlier this year in Sweden, which also has strict hate-crimes laws, a pastor was arrested at his church after he began reading Bible verses condemning homosexuality.

Some states have included sexual orientation in their state hate-crimes laws. Last month, California Gov. Arnold Schwarzenegger signed into law a bill expanding that state's statute to include not only homosexuals and transgendered people but also people who merely associate with those who are part of a protected class.

"While every hate crime represents a personal tragedy for the victim, hate crimes also are an attempt to intimidate a larger group or community of people," the bills' author, Senator Sheila Kuehl, told 365gay.com. "Hate crimes tear at the fabric of our society and it is important that we have a strong and effective response to them."

In Pennsylvania pastors are concerned they could be targeted under that state's new hate-crimes law, which added "sexual orientation" and "gender identity" as motives that trigger heavier penalties for the crime of "harassment."

Christ declared that in the last days, believers, firm in the gospel that men should repent of their sins, would be brought before governors for his sake, to be jailed, imprisoned and quite possibly killed for the gospel of Jesus Christ. How ironic that the very government meant to protect Godly virtues will be the very one that will persecute those who would promote said values this very nation was built upon.

To be clear, there is no other motivating factor for hatred other than the vocal resentment by traditional Christians who preach the gospel or support the view that the gay lifestyle is contrary to Biblical principals and those who participate in this lifestyle should be seen as people deceived into a sinful and wicked life. The fact is, the truth, the gospel truth will always be met with resentment and hatred.

One of the signs of the last days in which Christ warned us would come was immorality on a large scale and with that much persecution toward the church (saints). We are virtually seeing this especially here in the United States especially when it comes to sin and immorality – especially sexual immorality.

Notice the warning words of Christ, "Then shall they deliver you up to be afflicted, and shall kill you: and ye shall be hated of all nations for my name's sake." Matthew 24:9

Never before has there been such a time of hatred than in this current generation, but I would suggest that never a time is there a generation that is more wicked, more perverse than this generation. Why is it so great a darkened generation? It's because we are nearing the moment of the return of the King of Kings Jesus Christ.

The fact is this, since the early 1960's this nation has seen an ever decree of sinful behavior and resentment for the things of God. But the one main particular emphasis that accompanied other bad behaviors was the sin of sexual immorality.

With the explosion of the sexual revolution came with it, in my opinion, a demonic presence that captured the heart of the American youth and with it released a spirit of wickedness that had been unseen since the times of the Roman Empire as well as those fallen cities of Biblical times.

It has been said that, "When you coordinate and liberate and release the sexuality and the minds of youth, and can twist it and change it toward a different goal and direction, via rock 'n roll, via **ing in the streets, via dope, via action, direct action ... then you can maybe push this country and we can rewrite the whole structure, based on the kind of energy released by rock 'n roll." - Ed Sanders

Alfred Kinsey once stated, "The only unnatural sexual act is that which you cannot perform."

The 60's began the shift of a moral decline in morality in the United States as young people began to explore their sexuality thru every possible measure and with it came the entrance into the homosexual experience for many as men and women during this season age of "Aquarius" came out of the closet having been introduced to a new form of sexual exploration.

The permissive and persuasive spirit of deception and immoral behavior transpired throughout the nation during this time and from such the message was loud and clear, "If it feels good, do it."

The blinders of many were removed, as if by some desire to fulfill their own lust of the flesh and through this course of events they were carried away by their own passions because their heart was/is evil.

This is what James explained to us in James 1: 14-15, "But each one is tempted when he is carried away and enticed by his own lust. Then when lust has conceived, it gives birth to sin; and when sin is accomplished, it brings forth death."

This permissive acceptance of sin and immorality must always be challenged, especially in the time in which we live; there is none other like it that we can look to other than to those civilizations who forsook God and his commandments. The challenge since then is to preach the cross. But it is this message of the cross many do not, nor wish or want to hear.

The lines have been drawn and the message is clear, if we as believers are going to stand for Christ and for his glory then it is we who are going to face an unparallel attack in these last days for what we believe and stand for. I must make this clear; Satan realizes that his time is short, not for him only but for this present world. It is within this awareness that men and women of God must take a stand to what is right and Godly. We must not remain silent any longer. Yes, we do all things in love as believers, but we must tell those who are caught up into this lifestyle as well as so many other sins that there is hope, that there is a way out if they so desire it and that is thru the atoning blood of Jesus Christ and what he did on the cross.

But just as we as Christians have set our eyes upon the cross and for the challenge ahead, there is also another army, one whose sole mission is to destroy that which God has established the message of deliverance it is the army which Satan himself is leading the charge. There is an overwhelming hatred for the gospel these days, especially for those who support and promote traditional marriage. The reason is simple, darkness and those who are in it hate anything to do with the gospel of Jesus Christ. It is the gospel of the cross that pierces the darkness and the hearts of sinful man and many resent and abhor that which is good so they attack and persecute those who would dare share the gospel of peace and love.

This is the place where we are at, as men, determined to live the way they want, are intent on protecting and even promoting their way of life and if this means to silence those who would oppose such views then this would be simply a fulfilling of both agenda as well as prophecy.

Of course we are to love those that persecute us, we are to pray for our enemies, but at times it can become very difficult to pray for those who would attack a person simply based on their religious beliefs, but it's not so much the Christian as it's more of the Christian message that those in darkness hate to hear. This is where we are at in our society and I fear that as the days grow darker and the age in which we live begin to wrap up in Biblical fashion, we will see more and more of these sorts of attacks come on us. To be sure, there are going to be attacks upon the Christian in this great nation of ours, but it's simply a sign of the soon appearing of our Lord and savior.

I believe with the impending hate crime law this current administration (Obama Administration) is promoting along with the wave of anti-Christian intolerance rhetoric, we will see laws established that both promote as well as protect lifestyles which God has throughout time declared to be wicked and abhorred. As long as evil men who are placed in position of leadership under the disguise of "change" support or encourage laws that not only protects bad behavior but actually encourages it, then that nation and its people who support bad legislation and forget God will reap the consequences of sin.

Rome, Europe, Sodom all saw the hand of God upon their land, are we that different? The fact is, the times in which we are living demand that the church once again rise from its slumber and declare the glory of God and his righteousness. Regardless of the risk from what man can do, we as believers must come together under one voice and declare the word of God, that sin will keep one from heaven, that homosexuality, regardless of its popularity and quickly growing acceptance by our society, is nothing more than wicked, perverted behavior that God will demand payment for all those who partake in this abominable form of perversion. Even if this means persecution by our own governing laws, we as true believers must stand for the word of God, he expects no less than his children to declare that which is right and holy.

Chapter Nine

Apologizing for sin

He pastors one of the largest evangelical churches in America. His 2002 book, "The Purpose Driven Life" was a New York Times best seller and introduced the church world into a new age way of thinking that hundreds if not thousands of pastors and preachers have been indoctrinated with its teachings. Everything Rick Warren says is a compromise with the world instead of presenting the gospel of salvation to the world. But it's what he said on Larry King that shocked much of the evangelical church.

"You know, Larry, there was a story within a story that never got told," he said. "In the first place, I am not an anti-gay or anti-gay marriage activist. I never have been, never will be. During the whole Proposition 8 thing, I never once went to a meeting, never once issued a statement, never – never once even gave an endorsement in the two years Prop 8 was going. The week before the – the vote, somebody in my church said, Pastor Rick, what – what do you think about this? And I sent a note to my own members that said, I actually believe that marriage is – really should be defined, that that definition should be – say between a man and a woman.

"And then all of a sudden out of it, they made me, you know, something that I really wasn't," Warren continued. "And I actually – there were a number of things that were put out. I wrote to all my gay friends – the leaders that I knew – and actually apologized to them. That never got out. There were some things said that – you know, everybody should have 10 percent grace when they say public statements. And I was asked a question that made it sound like I equated gay marriage with pedophilia or incest, which I absolutely do not believe. And I actually announced that. All of the criticism came from people that didn't know me. Not a single criticism came from any gay leader who knows me and knows that for years, we've been working together on AIDS issues and all these other things." Rick Warren on the Larry King Show.

Warren is a great illustration of America's most prominent church leader backtracking and saying almost nothing coherent so that he will offend no one. He apologizes for the fact that at one time in his ministry he endorsed Proposition 8, which stated that marriage was between one man and one woman, but just like many who have decided to make friends with the world, Warren as well as others, have developed a position that says to support anything that offends the sinner, that calls for those in darkness to repent, is a position to be ignored and avoided – at any cost.

If a Christian pastor cannot stand up for clear teachings of their faith he certainly should not be standing in the pulpit. It is amazing to me that a "Evangelical" Christian leader would actually apologize to homosexual leaders because some of them might think he took the biblical stand against homosexual perversion and marriage perversion. But this is the real issue of the church – it has become lukewarm and apologetic in these last days!

The issue is; why does the church feel the need to apologize for its belief? Have we become ashamed of the gospel, especially the gospel of condemnation? Have we as the church reached a point in our spiritual and moral failure to hold to that which is true? I believe the answer is – yes we have!

I recall watching a national political talk show host recently and he made the comment why is there so much evil in the world, homosexuality, child abuse and the growing of immorality in America. I thought about what he said and suddenly I realized what the Holy Spirit was telling me, the answer was simple and clear, the church has lost its grip on our society and culture.

The main reason that there is so much immorality and perversion taking place in our nation is due to the fact that the church has failed to preach the gospel of Jesus Christ! This is the only true answer we as believers who understand what's taking place in our nation can come up with. I've often said that one can tell the condition of the church by looking at the nation. The reason? We are salt. Christ told us that we are to be salt to the world, but for many today the church has all but lost its salt, its ability to bring about condemnation to those acts of sin that society is endorsing. When the church of Jesus Christ fails to condemn sin, when it fails to condemn open rebellion then one can readily prepare for the failure of that nation.

The other problem the church has had recently is that it has tried to make peace with the world. How many times have I as a preacher encountered believers who claim Christ, yet they admonish anyone who would dare preach against sinners in a way that is not non judging. There is this idea that says we are not to judge, I hear it all the time and I am sure most readers of this book hear it all too often themselves. This is also a ploy the enemy uses to disrupt the preaching of the gospel to those who are bound in sin.

The argument many spout is why preach against sinners and their condition when we should just love them and let them live their life accordingly? The answer is clear, Jesus called us to preach the gospel, call sinners to repentance and baptize them. We are to bring them out of the darkness that they are in, but in order for us to show them the light of truth, we must always condemn their actions.

I often tell the story when I argue with these liberal Christians who have this deluded idea that we should not preach against sin, that a young man walked into a doctors office, he was in terrible pain which was obvious but he didn't know exactly what was wrong with him. The nurse came in and walked him back into one of the many rooms for patients and proceeded to take his blood pressure and asked him several questions then proceeded to tell him to undress and the doctor would be in soon the meet with him to see what exactly was going on. When the doctor came in, he examined the young man and realized that he was in all actuality a very sick young man. After doing several tests, the doctor realized to his sadness that the young man showed signs of cancer; it was in the second stage.

The doctor, overcome with grief and despair to have to tell this young man who was in the prime of his life that he was dying of Cancer, came into the office and met the man and began to speak with him. He then informed him that he simply was sick and to take a couple of aspirins and sent him home believing that dishonesty and not wanting to judge his true condition was much better than condemning the young man to death.

The sad fact is, the church is doing the very same thing to those who are lost without Christ!

The church has failed miserably to preach the gospel to the lost and instead has adopted the unscriptural theology that silence is better than judging. And let me be clear on this matter of judging. We are called to judge that which sin is. The idea that we as the church can remain silent when it comes to sin is literally sending millions to hell simply because we desire to save a persons feelings from being hurt! This is not the gospel of Christ.

The apostle Paul made it very clear to the Corinth church that there was a young man involved in a sexual affair, he had received word that the church had not openly rebuked this young man and that by remaining silent they were just as guilty as this young man who was sleeping with his fathers wife, the young man's step mother!

The apostle Paul demanded one immediate course to take – expose this sin that was taking place and remove him from the church, giving him over to Satan to do with whatever he pleased with him. Now, to many this might seem harsh and not politically correct. After all, could one imagine in today's world what would come of someone being challenged in church that their conduct was bringing harm against the body of Christ and that by allowing such bad behavior that they were allowing Satan to destroy the work of God?

Paul's declaration was then made clear when it came to such lifestyles, "Know ye not that the unrighteous shall not inherit the kingdom of God? Be not deceived: neither fornicators, nor idolaters, nor adulterers, nor effeminate, nor abusers of themselves with mankind, nor thieves, nor covetous, nor drunkards, nor revilers, nor extortioners, shall inherit the kingdom of God." 1st. Corinthians 6: 9-10

This is where we are at when it comes to our society, we have become immune to the sin that is being propagated in our culture and have become desensitized to what we see and hear taking place in our land. The chief reason being is because we don't want to offend anyone. But the gospel will always offend, we might not offend, we might take another course and play nice, but the word of God will always offend the wicked!

Sadly, there are a great many churches today where unbelievers remain unconverted, attending weekly, and never finding anything offensive about the message that's preached. Pastors who, for fear of losing congregations as well as finances, will not preach the full gospel of Jesus Christ and will refrain from preaching against immorality and sin. Many preachers today have all but put down the word of God and have replaced it with self help books, books about living your best life today and how to be prosperous and attain great wealth. The gospel has been overcome with political ideology instead of spirituality of holiness living and spiritual separation from the world.

But Charles Spurgeon reminds us that . . .

There are some who stumble at Christ because of his holiness. He is too strict for them; they would like to be Christians, but they cannot renounce their sensual pleasures; they would like to be washed in his blood, but they desire still to roll in the mire of sin.

Willing enough the mass of men would be to receive Christ, if, after receiving him, they might continue in their drunkenness, their wantonness, and self-indulgence. But Christ lays the axe at the root of the tree; he tells them that these things must be given up, for "because of these things the wrath of God comes upon the children of disobedience", and "without holiness no man can see the Lord". Human nature kicks at this.

"What! May I not enjoy one darling lust? May I not indulge myself at least now and then in these things? Must I altogether forsake my old habits and my old ways? Must I be made a new creature in Christ Jesus?"

These are terms too hard, conditions too severe, and so the human heart goes back to the flesh pots of Egypt, and clings to the garlic and the onions of the old estate of bondage, and will not be set free even though a greater than Moses lifts up the rod to part the sea, and promises to give to them a Canaan flowing with milk and honey. Christ offends men because his gospel is intolerant of sin.

The real problem is we have become tolerant to sin and we refuse to acknowledge that Christ has called us to admonish those in darkness, to compel them to come in and be saved. The truth offends most people, but the Word of God teaches that we should LOVE THE TRUTH. "And with all deceivableness of unrighteousness in them that perish; because they received not the love of the truth, that they might be saved." -2nd Thessalonians 2:10.

It's not the homosexual that we despise, far from it, but it's the ACT and the promotion of this sin that we as believers must always come against. To be clear, the challenge in these last days will be one of great hardship for the church of God. The church must realize that it must return to the values of what it was founded on, the principals of Jesus Christ and when we accept those principals then we will be a powerful force against the forces of darkness.

The Gospel of Jesus Christ Has Always Offended the Wicked! Romans 9:33 refers to Christ as a "stumblingblock" and a "Rock of offence." Jesus clearly taught in Matthew 10: 34, 35 that He did NOT come to this world to bring peace. Let me clarify, Jesus' did come to die upon the cross for our sins; thus, enabling us to have peace with God through the precious shed blood of Jesus Christ. BUT, Jesus also expects us to preach the Gospel, which OFFENDS most people. Let me define "Gospel" so there is no misunderstanding. 1st Corinthians 15:1-4 defines the "Gospel" as the DEATH, BURIAL, and RESURRECTION of Christ Jesus. This includes the blood of Jesus Christ (Romans 5:9). Without the shedding of blood, there is no remission of sin (Hebrews 9:22; Revelation 7:14).

When I was growing up in Muncie, Indiana, my family would go to our little church on the south side of Muncie and there we would hear the gospel being preached as it should be, with full conviction and full force. But as time passed and people became more settled (comfortable) with life, careers, family, etc, etc, there was a clear mark of change that began to take place. It was subtle at first, but as time began to pass and people's ideas and beliefs began to grow distant from the truth, things began to change and not for the better. Not wanting to sound legalistic, but there were stark ideas being promoted that were simply contrary to the full gospel of Christ. A more liberal overtone was beginning to take shape that said that the ideas of the old were not exactly correct, that one could partake of the world's system, it's entertainment, it's "fun" it's gambling casinos, it's idolization of sports and Hollywood celebrities as well as the acceptance of the world's music. All began to surface from the pulpit on down. Even the power of God was beginning to depart in many ways.

Growing up Pentecostal, I was witnessed to several of the old fashioned meetings throughout the south. I can still recall being taken by my mother at the age of 5 and 6 years of age to old fashioned camp meetings where I witnessed people shouting, miracles taking place, sinners coming to the alter. I recall my parents telling me along with their friends how drunks would stumble into the services, only to feel the overpowering conviction of the holy spirit drawing them to an old fashioned alter and there they would find the peace and joy and love they were looking for rather than thru a bottle. They found Christ! And not only did they find Christ, they were completely made sober from the moment they rose from that hay covered dirt ground.

That was the power of God that was taking place, but as I grew older that same power was being taken out, not by God's will or desire but by the church! What had started to occur was that many pastors began to apologize for the acts of the past. They had become indoctrinated by the psychology of the day, where they would rather use the wisdom of men than the power of God. Soon, more and more ideas of the past, holiness teachings were being replaced by the appeal of psychology and sociology and the mind rather than the wisdom of the word of God.

This is where we are currently in our nation and the world. When the church conforms to be like the world, when Christians declare themselves to be seeker friendly Christians and no longer judge that which is evil, when believers no longer call sinners to repentance the outcome is chaos.

The church has become apologetic in these last days. The root of

America's ills is its apostate church leaders.

Preaching against sin is at the very core of the true Christian faith. Without preaching against sin, there is no conviction, and without conviction there is no repentance. This is the main problem in America today, and the reason why America is so messed up--because preachers have stopped preaching against sin! Go to the average so-called "church" today and you won't hear anything negative said about abortion, divorce, homosexuality, pornography, gambling, booze, hellivision, Freemasonry, false religion, movies, rock music, witchcraft, etc. And then the few churches that do preach against sin, never take the message outside the church walls, operating more like the occult than a church. The word "occult" means "to hide from view." Most churches have their little "click" of people, and it's nothing more than a social club. When they do meet together, they criticize other Christians who are serving the Lord. Every church should be known in their local community as a sin-fighting church, and a charitable church, and a soul winning church, etc.

We must call sinners to repentance, we must tell the homosexual that in God's eyes, this lifestyle is an abomination and those who willfully commit these terrible acts face judgment by an almighty God. This is the gospel that we need to start preaching once again and get away from this new "social" gospel that is plaguing so many of our churches pulpits and have deceived many into thinking that their life choices are not "alternative" but condemned by God. There is a better way and that is thru Jesus Christ and what he did on the cross.

Let's start preaching the gospel and stop apologizing for it!

"Old-fashioned, Spirit-filled, Christ-honoring, sin-hating, soul-winning, Bible preaching! It is the hope of the church! It is the hope of the nation! It is the hope of the world!"

-Pastor Jack Hyles

Chapter Ten

A President's agenda

Something's bugging me and I can't let it go. It basically started yesterday evening and lasted throughout most of the night. No, it wasn't indigestion, wasn't GURD, it was something else that I could not let go of until I found myself doing some research. Then I found it, it was the connection I had been searching for and it was startling.

For years the homosexual camp in America has long desired to get a foothold into our culture but they were, for the most part, regulated to the Colleges and Universities of our educational system, where, without fear of being singled out and thrown back into the closet, they could cultivate and indoctrinate the young minds that came into their social web of deceit. But then the times began to change and the invidual gay man or woman became bolder and more vocal in larger numbers and they were not satisfied with just one small aspect of our society, they wanted more and they came up with a game plan to make their perversion more acceptable in our culture like never before.

It didn't take long till the gay activist and their agenda took other areas of relevance in our culture, from books to movies to television, especially in pop music. Pop icons such as Lady Ga Ga, an openly bi sexual woman and Katy Perry, who just recently announced that she is also bi sexual, and I might add is a former pentecostal christian who was raised in a pentecostal church. The fact is, the homosexual defenders maintained a certain control, but it wasn't until recently that they had snagged the biggest gift of all time to further their political social agenda - the White House.

There has never been a time in our society where any particular group or people has been given a literal pass into one of the most trusted places of leadership than the homosexual organization has been given under the current Presidency of one Barack Obama.

From Obama's mysterious and unexplained relationship with one Larry Sinclair who, for a brief time, revealed that he and then University student Obama, had a brief, one time sexual relationship but was quickly silenced, to Obama's campaign organizer and now czar over the national public education system - Kevin Jennings.

The fact is, there are serious questions just why Obama has maintained a close relationship with the homosexual movement. But it's very obvious to me why he maintains such a close association to these men and women - he's gay himself and he supports their agenda. There is no other way one can explain his sympathetic nature to this part of our growing segment in our nation other than he himself is a gay man.

So, let's look at who Barrack Obama aligns himself with and then you decide for yourself if you come away with the same conclusion.

Kevin Jennings. Jennings is the founder of GLSEN -- the Gay, Lesbian, and Straight Education Network. This is the same Kevin Jennings who you have to thank for the fact that "gay" clubs exist in many schools across the country today. Also thanks to Jennings, GLSEN sponsors the so-called "Day of Silence" in thousands of schools across America, when students are encouraged to take a vow of silence to show solidarity with their LGBT (lesbian, gay, bisexual, transgendered) classmates. And courtesy of GLSEN's website, you can get a list of recommended books for every age group, starting with kindergarten, to introduce children to the subject of homosexuality.

In Massachusetts, GLSEN is famous (or infamous) for what's become known as "fistgate." And here's where the distasteful part begins. On March 25, 2000, GLSEN sponsored, along with the Massachusetts Department of Education, a taxpayer-funded conference. Its goals included putting Gay/Straight Alliances into more Massachusetts schools, and expanding homosexual teaching into lower grades.

Many gay-friendly teachers (who received development credits for being there) and administrators attended, along with students who were bussed in from their home districts.

One particular workshop was listed as a "youth only, ages 14-21" session, run by three self-professed gay presenters. Thanks to two members of a local Parents' Rights Coalition who secretly taped the session, we know exactly what happened. One of the teachers asked the assembled students what "fisting" meant. Following a descriptive definition, another of the adult presenters proceeded to demonstrate the proper formation of the hand for this sexual act. After a student of about 16 said that it didn't sound very appealing, the third adult presenter calmed his concerns. This technique, she explained, "often gets a really bad rap," and that it was "an experience of letting somebody into your body that you want to be that close and intimate with." Other homosexual acts were discussed and described in detail.

In 2002, GLSEN sponsored another conference which included a seminar on "Gender in the Early Childhood Classroom" which explored ways of setting "the tone for nontraditional gender role play" for preschoolers. Remember, it is Kevin Jennings who created this group, which is run by the current Administration under his leadership and receives Government funding.

So why would President Obama devote so much time associating with these people who are adament in indoctrinating our children as young as 5 with the gay and lesbian concept and beliefs? Let's read from Obama's own words in a speech in August 2008. "I believe we can achieve equality for the millions of the LGBT people in this country, and with this team [LGBT] I know that the LGBT community will play a major role in our campaign to bring change to Washington."

So, it was very clear during the campaign that Obama had a personal stake in the moving in of the homosexual agenda into our schools, he wasn't happy with just its influence in our culture thru media, he wanted, along with others, a more effective imprint of this philosophy in the hearts and minds of our children. I repeat, there is no other prupose or reason for his staunch support other than Barack Obama is a closet homosexual in his heart.

In March of 1995 to the Human Rights Campaign Fund Leadership Conference called "Winning the Culture War." Here's a small portion of what he said: "In Massachusetts the effective reframing of this issue was the key to the success of the Governor's Commission on Gay and Lesbian Youth. We immediately seized upon the opponent's calling card – safety – and explained how homophobia represents a threat to students' safety by creating a climate where violence, name-calling, health problems, and suicide are common. Titling our report 'Making Schools Safe for Gay and Lesbian Youth,' we automatically threw our opponents onto the defensive and stole their best line of attack. This framing short-circuited their arguments and left them back-pedaling from day one."

Kevin Jennings wrote the foreword to the book *Queering Elementary Education*, which offers essays on "Locating a Place for Gay and Lesbian Themes in Elementary Reading, Writing and Talking." (Interestingly enough, Bill Ayers wrote a glowing blurb for the back of the book.)

The point is, why surround yourself with people who have a clear agenda other than you are apart of the same? The fact is, this President is sympathetic to homosexuals simply because he is one. There can be no other reason for his strange, abnormal behaviour other than he himself is gay or bi-sexual.

But let's look at one other recent endorsement of Obama.

President Obama's recess appointment of an outspoken supporter of gay rights to the Equal Employment Opportunity Commission is causing alarm among social conservatives, who worry that she'll strip religious rights from schools and businesses and "revolutionize" social norms in the workplace.

The appointment of Georgetown University Law Center Professor Chai Feldblum to be one of the EEOC's five commissioners went largely unnoticed on Saturday, as Republicans zeroed in on Obama's naming of pro-union labor lawyer Craig Becker to the National Labor Relations Board.

While Feldblum's work to end prejudice against gays and lesbians has been lauded by many in the legal community, conservative groups say her appointment to the EEOC will have detrimental and far-reaching consequences.

"She wants to change the moral bearing of this country," said Andrea Lafferty, executive director of the Traditional Values Coalition. Lafferty said the hiring of a transgender teacher in a school, for example, would be "traumatizing" for students who are "still growing and learning about sexuality."

"We send children to school to learn reading, writing and arithmetic. Having a transgender or 'she-male' teacher in the classroom should not be part of that equation," she said.

Feldblum's public comments and causes have raised alarm among social conservatives. In a 2004 speech at UCLA, she said "gay sex is morally good" and boasted about a project she launched, known as Workplace Flexibility 2010, which she said aimed to "change the face of the American workplace" and "revolutionize social norms."

The Obama administration is standing by its decision to appoint the Harvard-educated attorney to the EEOC, an independent federal agency that enforces laws against workplace discrimination.

The fact remains, this President, unlike any other President, has aligned himself with the gay movement an thus, bringing in his own anti-christian beliefs. Doesn't it make you wonder why this President still has not found a church as every other President has done? Does it not bring into question as to why this President has aligned himself with individuals who, by their own words and deeds, have an agenda of their own, to force the ideas of homosexuality upon the children of our nation?

There is no other explanation other than this President is a homosexual and a supporter of this lifestyle. From his own personal relationship with Larry Sinclair to both Obama and Rahm Emanuel who both frequented a well known gay bath house called "Man's Country" in Chicago when Obama was a then U.S. Senator. The homosexual vision for America's future is characteristically hedonistic and selfishly narcissistic, for it is defined by that which it opposes and seeks to destroy: Judeo-Christian family-based society. Although they are practised at making themselves appear to be victims, rather than aggressors, hatred toward the heterosexual community occupies a major role in the motivation of the Gay/Lesbian activist leadership

But I must remind those who continue to support this President of God's position on anyone wanting or living this lifestyle.

"Do you not know that the unrighteous will not inherit the kingdom of God? Do not be deceived. Neither fornicators, nor idolaters, nor adulterers, nor homosexuals, nor sodomites." 1 Cor. 6:9

Conclusion

From the pages of past history, man has always run against the will of God, in almost every concept and idea. His thirst for power and wealth has been his goal, but each and every time he reaches out to that which never seems to fit into his grasp, he always comes away empty for it rests in his immoral insight and his sin filled soul.

The truth is, God has established every people and it's nation how to walk and how to behave, it's called, most appropriately - the Ten Commandments. It is these commandments that God layed down that gives us insight on how to live, how to take care of others and how to worship God truthfully and sincerely.

But, as man turns his back on God and his virtues, all of mankind suffers, even nature itself also feels man's burdens due to his sin.

This is why Christ came and died, so that man could once again have purpose and meaning thru a personal relationship with Jesus Christ.

But man is once again rejecting that message, the message of the cross and is once again going down a road that will once again lead to destruction. The first destruction came thru the means of water (a flood) but the second will be thru fire.

America and the rest of the world is at a crossroads of eternal destination and it is that very dilemma that will send the world, once again on a course with its destiny - judgement.

Judgement is coming to our world for we have accepted everything God hates and calls sin. From killing our children to perversion, our world is calling evil good and good evil and now a verdict, long overdue, is about to be declared and sentencing imposed. Our only solution as Christians is to warn the lost of their unrighteousness, of what they are going to face and why this nation as well as much of the world is about to undergo a dramatic change.

The fact is, there is but only one hope for the world and that is repenting and bowing before Christ and accepting his mercy, but the sad truth remains, most will not accept this wonderful gift of salvation and thus, the sentence of judgment will begin.

Let us work while it is day, for the night is soon upon us that we cannot work. For this I say, "Come Lord Jesus".

Made in the USA
Lexington, KY
09 March 2013